A Devon House

The Story of Poltimore

Jocelyn Hemming

Edited by Peter Howard

University of Plymouth Press

Paperback edition first published in the UK in 2005 by
University of Plymouth Press,
in association with
Intellect Books, PO Box 862, Bristol BS99 1DE, UK.

Paperback edition first published in the USA in 2005 by
University of Plymouth Press,
in association with
Intellect Books, ISBS, 920 NE 58th Ave. Suite 300,
Portland, Oregon, USA.

Publishers: Jessica Garcia and Laura Gil

Cover design: Chris Durant

A catalogue record for this book is available from the British Library

ISBN 1-84150-935-3

Printed and bound by Orchard Press, UK

Contents

Foreword

I first saw Poltimore House on a summer's day. The approach through the rustling of green leaves and the fields of juicy grass was as lyrical as you could imagine. And the house when it came into view lived up to my expectations. The style of its architecture, the low line of its façade, the beautiful proportions of the windows combine to make the first impression one that raises the spirits.

The next moment the spirits sink. For, of course, this is now a building that has fallen into decay. Lying unused and with no upkeep to secure the walls and roof there has been massive damage. Vandals, with empty minds and no sense of their own heritage, have ransacked much of the interior. Yet this is a house that tells a long and beautiful story. And for that it is much cherished by those who value what it has been and might be once again.

So near to Exeter, it is not surprising that Poltimore House has played a part in its history and that of the South West. Once you step behind the façade, the richness of its past is revealed. Stepping over broken glass and rubble I exclaimed again and again at new and important disclosures. The remains of the original Tudor house are substantial and impressive. One can stand in what was once the courtyard and imagine the life that was lived there. The curving staircase is another delight. Even more is revealed in the interior. The rococo saloon must have been a dazzling sight in its heyday. The virtue of its proportions, the elegance of its mirrors and ceiling shine through the grime and decay. There is something transcendent about beauty that defies time to do its worst. Along the broad and handsome corridors and into the fine rooms along the front of the house, the legacy of architectural poise and elegance survives the dereliction.

The hand of time has to be stayed. Left without care, this lovely house will deteriorate beyond a point of no return. And those who created it, those who have cherished it over the centuries, those who lived here as family, those who were educated here as pupils, those mothers who gave birth to their children here, will have something they cherished wiped out leaving only fading memories behind.

Why should this matter? Plenty of us think it does. The heritage of our and every country is precious because it charts the imprint made by the human race on the history of the planet. People from the South Seas, or the North Pole, from the heart of Asia, and from the depths of tropical jungles, all pay homage to what has gone before. There is no tribe or people, no race or culture that does not respect its ancestors and seek to keep their memory alive. Poltimore House is a small part of our memory, a small and beautiful part of southwest England that tells of its past, records its beauty and deserves to serve its future.

Joan Bakewell
December, 2004

THE BAMPFYLDE FAMILY FROM THE LATE 15TH CENTURY

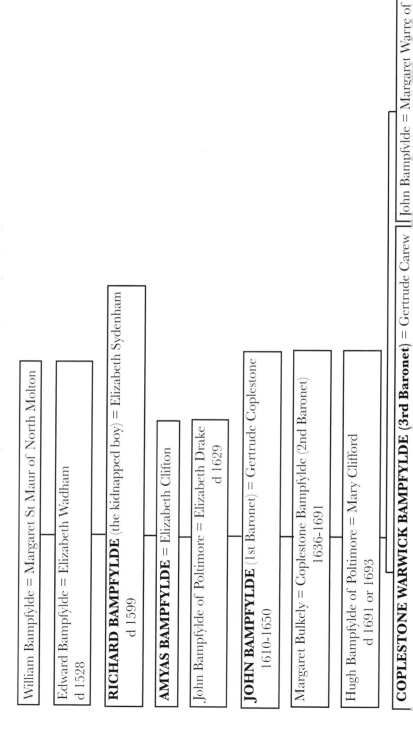

William Bampfylde = Margaret St Maur of North Molton

Edward Bampfylde = Elizabeth Wadham
d 1528

RICHARD BAMPFYLDE (the kidnapped boy) = Elizabeth Sydenham
d 1599

AMYAS BAMPFYLDE = Elizabeth Clifton

John Bampfylde of Poltimore = Elizabeth Drake
d 1629

JOHN BAMPFYLDE (1st Baronet) = Gertrude Coplestone
1610-1650

Margaret Bulkely = Coplestone Bampfylde (2nd Baronet)
1636-1691

Hugh Bampfylde of Poltimore = Mary Clifford
d 1691 or 1693

COPLESTONE WARWICK BAMPFYLDE (3rd Baronet) = Gertrude Carew ‖ John Bampfylde = Margaret Warre of

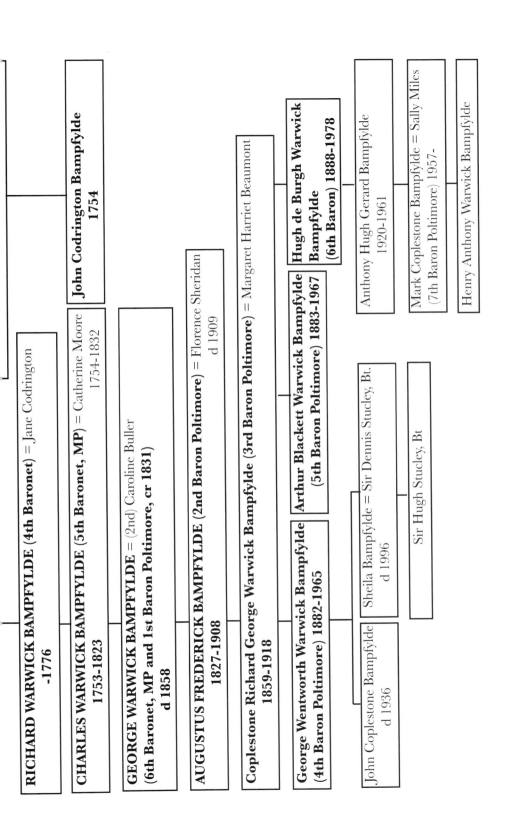

RICHARD WARWICK BAMPFYLDE (4th Baronet) = Jane Codrington
-1776

John Codrington Bampfylde
1754

CHARLES WARWICK BAMPFYLDE (5th Baronet, MP) = Catherine Moore
1753-1823   1754-1832

GEORGE WARWICK BAMPFYLDE = (2nd) Caroline Buller
(6th Baronet, MP and 1st Baron Poltimore, cr 1831)
d 1858

AUGUSTUS FREDERICK BAMPFYLDE (2nd Baron Poltimore) = Florence Sheridan
1827-1908   d 1909

Coplestone Richard George Warwick Bampfylde (3rd Baron Poltimore) = Margaret Harriet Beaumont
1859-1918

Arthur Blackett Warwick Bampfylde
(5th Baron Poltimore) 1883-1967

Hugh de Burgh Warwick
Bampfylde
(6th Baron) 1888-1978

George Wentworth Warwick Bampfylde
(4th Baron Poltimore) 1882-1965

Sheila Bampfylde = Sir Dennis Stucley, Bt.
d 1996

Anthony Hugh Gerard Bampfylde
1920-1961

John Coplestone Bampfylde
d 1936

Sir Hugh Stucley, Bt

Mark Coplestone Bampfylde = Sally Miles
(7th Baron Poltimore) 1957-

Henry Anthony Warwick Bampfylde

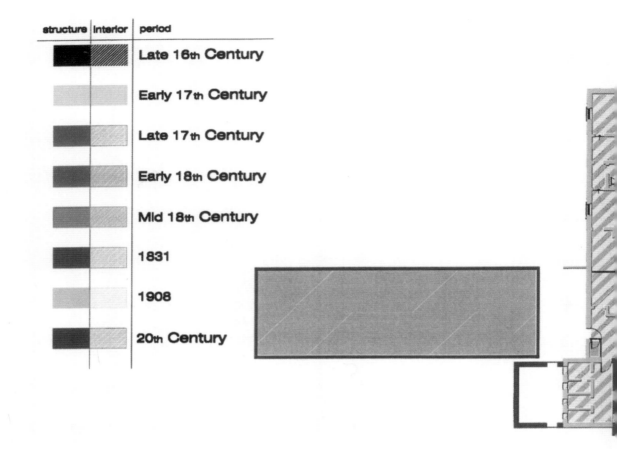

structure	interior	period
		Late 16th Century
		Early 17th Century
		Late 17th Century
		Early 18th Century
		Mid 18th Century
		1831
		1908
		20th Century

0 1 2 3 4 5   10   20 Metres

Scale

POLTIMORE HOUSE - Historical Development
Ground Floor Plan

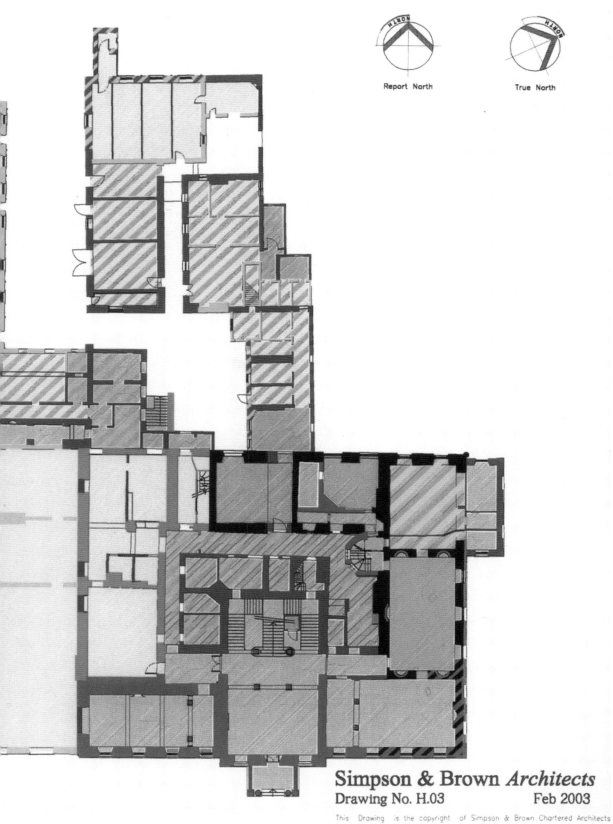

Report North

True North

Simpson & Brown *Architects*
Drawing No. H.03   Feb 2003

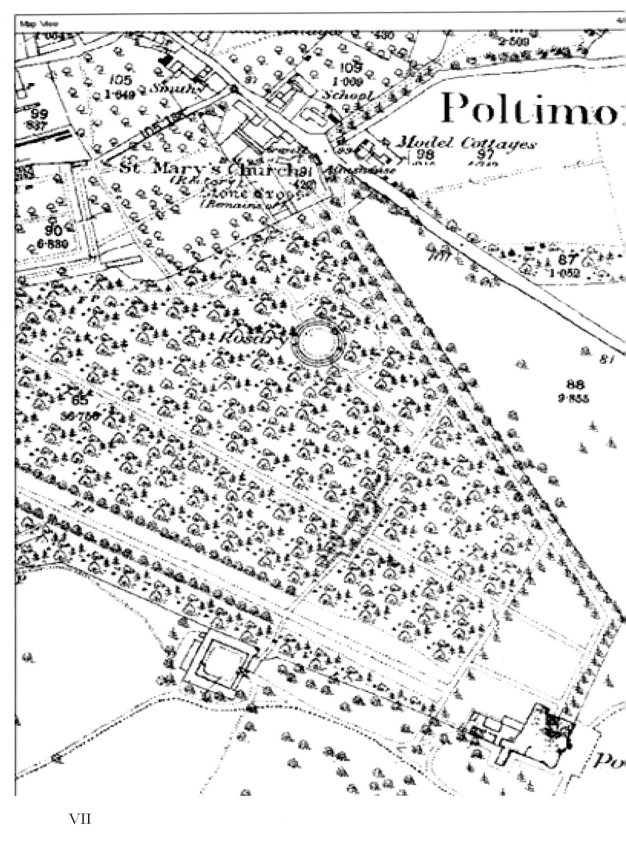

VII

Introduction

To tell the story of any great house inevitably involves the story of the people who built and owned it, perhaps over many generations. In the case of Poltimore House this is certainly true; one family, the Bampfyldes, having held the land on which the house was built for over 600 years from the reign of Edward I to the first quarter of the 20th century. Their history is bound up with the progression of the house from 16th-century manorial dwelling to stately 20th-century mansion, the centre of a very large Devonshire estate. What happened in the decades after 1920 is the story of many other people to whom the house meant not just home, but learning, livelihood and new life—and is a story that continues to this day.

My connections with Poltimore House go back to the years before the Second World War. For my sisters and I, living a few miles away, with school friends to visit at Huxham and Stoke Canon, it was a short detour on the way home to go through Poltimore village and down the hill to the deer park. The deer were the object of our interest, and we used to hang on the railings by Old Lodge and watch the big herd with broad antlers and spotted coats that grazed under the spreading oaks. The park was more thickly wooded then, the house barely glimpsed through the trees—a distant, pale building of no particular concern to us. The Bampfyldes had not long left Poltimore, and we knew only that it was a school for girls with whom we had no contact. The war came; the girls' school went, there were no deer to be visited, and then ninety boys from Dover arrived at the house for the duration. Later, our parents bought Poltimore

OPPOSITE

A map of Poltimore dated 1880

VIII

House and converted it into the first of the post-war hospitals, and a medical establishment it remained for the next thirty years.

Since then it has been a great privilege to meet and correspond with many former pupils of Poltimore College and Dover College, and with former hospital staff, with patients and with descendants of those who worked at Poltimore in the early years of the 20th century. Indeed this book would only be half written were it not for the cooperation and willingness to share their memories and in many cases to provide valuable written reminiscences, letters and photographs.

Only a handful of images of Poltimore House exist from the pre-photography era. The aquatint of the south front and deer park in 1827 is now well known, but there are no paintings of the house so far as can be ascertained. The earliest impressions of what it may have looked like over a century after it was built come from three drawings of 1716 and 1727 by the topographical artist Edmund Prideaux. These drawings are reproduced by courtesy of the Society of Architectural Historians of Great Britain from Vol. VII of their Journal. Thanks also to the Prideaux-Brune family for permission to inspect the originals at Prideaux Place in Cornwall. Other travelling artists seem to have passed Poltimore by; even that inveterate recorder of country houses of the late 18th century, the Reverend John Swete, who shamelessly sponged on the owners of large estates for his bed and board in return for a watercolour or two, declared that he, 'had not a word to say in regard to the grounds or park which has few, if any, circumstances of local or adventitious beauty to recommend it'. But then, he may not have found the owner at home ready to dispense the legendary Bampfylde hospitality!

In writing of Poltimore House through the ages, therefore, it is inevitable that the words 'may be', 'possibly' or 'probably' are repeated in the telling of it; there simply is no certainty about the extent of the Tudor building, of how the interior was arranged until the 19th-century photographs reveal the layout of the principal rooms, or of any clear indication of the landscaping, or lack of landscaping, of the estate. But while there may be shadows in the corners and gaps in our knowledge regarding successive rebuildings and refurbishings by the Bampfyldes of their great house, it is fortunate that many of their portraits survive. Poltimore House Trust is greatly indebted to Sir Hugh Stucley, Bt, DL and Mrs Sally Worthington, grandson and granddaughter of the 4th Baron Poltimore, for giving Dick Brownridge unlimited access for photography, and permission to reproduce the portraits of the Bampfylde family featured in this book. Many of these paintings, which once hung in Poltimore House, can now be seen at Hartland Abbey in North Devon, which is open to the public for part of the year,

The sources used in this book are numerous, both written and verbal. The thanks of the Trust and the author go out to all these people, and many more who have given freely of their time, knowledge and talents to help both this book and the future of the house and grounds.

Finally I owe a great deal to the meticulous research carried out by my father when he was writing his booklet in retirement in the 1970s—*From Celtic Settlement to 20th-Century Hospital: the story of Poltimore House*. I have drawn on this publication for many sources.

Jocelyn Hemming
Cadbury, 2004

Invaders, a Kidnapping and a Charitable Deed: 100 BC–AD 1600

A few miles north of Exeter on the level land between the rivers Exe and Clyst a large, white-stuccoed house stands four-square and solid against a background of dark trees. 'A plain mansion in a dull park' is how W.G. Hoskins described it in his book *Devon,* although Nikolaus Pevsner and Bridget Cherry in *The Buildings of England* wrote a great deal more enthusiastically; and Simon Jenkins in his magisterial *England's Thousand Best Houses* includes it, considering its ruinous state, 'out of expectation'. Admittedly, at first sight, seen briefly by those speeding along the M5 motorway a few hundred yards away, the long, regular line of unadorned windows, and heavy porch give no hint of what might lie behind the façade, or any inkling of Poltimore's colourful history. The parkland in front was once more thickly wooded, with fine spreading oaks and a roaming herd of fallow deer, one of only a few in Devon. Now the deer have gone and the park is sadly thinned, but across the lawns east of the house the celebrated avenue of lime trees still marks the path to the church and village of Poltimore.

For over six centuries the Bampfylde family lived at Poltimore, and every hundred years or so successive generations pulled down and rebuilt or extended the mansion and modernised their estate. The result is a complex architectural jigsaw, some elements of which remain unresolved today. When the Bampfyldes left in 1921 the house, by then considered too big for private use, became first a school and then a hospital until, after a series of unfortunate ownerships, it suffered the chaos resulting from repossession, arson,

OPPOSITE
The park from an upstairs window

2

vandalism, theft and chronic neglect before its rescue in 1996.

To go back to the beginning, Devon (and Cornwall) were occupied in the late Iron Age by the Dumnonii, a Celtic tribe, whose name was used by the Romans when they founded the city of Exeter and called it Isca Dumnoniorum. Roman coins were dug up in a potato field in Poltimore parish in 1838, but signs of Roman occupation in the area are few, although it is fairly established that they took over the Iron Age fort on Stoke Hill and may have had an outpost a few miles away at Killerton. Six centuries then passed before the Saxons arrived in this part of England, after which a relative peace descended until the Viking invasions began in AD 871. Devon was constantly raided, and in 1001 the Saxons fought (and lost) against the Danes in a battle at Pinhoe. Broadclyst and neighbouring villages, including Poltimore, were probably sacked. There is no archaeological evidence for this event but the names of Danes Hill and Dandy Lane, both near Poltimore, reinforce the tradition. It thus remained for the Norman invaders later to set some sort of stamp on the ownership and use of the land. In the Domesday Survey two manors were recorded at Poltimore, the main one held by Haemeric de Arcis, an officer in the army of William I, and a smaller one, Cutton (a farm today), between Poltimore and Killerton, which belonged to the Canons of St Mary at Rouen.

The name Poltimore itself may derive from a Celtic root—in Old Welsh, Pwll-ty-mawr (Pwyll, pool; Ty, house; and Mawr, great) or 'the Pool by the Great House'. The de Pultymor family, probably of Norman descent, who owned the manor of Poltimore in the 13th century also held land at a place called Poltimore in Glamorgan, although it is not known whether they took their name from the Devon or the Welsh lands.

Nothing exists today to show a Norman presence in Poltimore village except the font in the church of St Mary, a red sandstone building erected by the Bampfyldes in the 14th century that may have replaced an earlier one on the site. The first record relating to Poltimore after Domesday is in the Devon Assize Rolls of 1218 –19 where Stephen de Pultymor put in a claim against Roger de Lymburg (Lymbury, in Broadclyst parish, known today as Reed's Cottages) for causing an annoyance to his tenants by diverting a stream. Stephen's heirs retained the manor until 1293. It was then given to Simon de Montacute who very soon disposed of it to William Pontyngton, a Canon of Exeter Cathedral. The new owner

did not hold the estate for long and in 1298 bequeathed it to his pupil John Bampfylde, of Weston (now Weston Bampfylde) in Dorset.

John, the first Bampfylde to own the land at Poltimore, was himself the son of a John Bampfylde, and his successors were John, Thomas, John, Thomas, John and John, followed by William, Walter and William and then Edward. During this long period from 1298 the family acquired other lands by marriage to the St Maurs at North Molton in Devon and the Pedertons of Hardington in Somerset, and thereby gained a certain position in the county. In 1324 in the reign of Edward II, John de Bamfield of Poltimore is recorded in Palgrave's Parliamentary Writs as one of the 'men at arms' liable for military service against the Scots, while a later John Bampfylde in the 15th century was made Crown Escheator for Devon and Cornwall. Given their status in Devon during this time it is likely that the Bampfyldes lived at Poltimore, although there is today no trace of any medieval house built by them on the site of the present mansion. However, 'Town orchard' is recorded on the tithe map of 1841 on the high ground near the church and next to the oldest house in the village

ABOVE

Fallow deer in the park

4

ABOVE

The northeast front of Poltimore House in 1716 as drawn by Edmund Prideaux

(formerly Cross Cottage, now Towan House). This may have been the demesne farm of the lord of the manor where the Bampfyldes lived for the first two and a half centuries after they inherited the Poltimore estate. Their house may even be the dwelling shown on Saxton's Map of 1575, when Poltimore was first recorded as a fenced deer park.

However, on the death of Edward Bampfylde in 1528, the whole estate was very nearly lost. Edward's two-year-old son Richard, heir to both the Poltimore and North Molton lands, was supposedly kidnapped and taken out of Devon, leaving the properties in the hands of trustees who quarrelled violently about their shares in the estate. One version of this rather romantic story is that the child was brought up as his kidnapper's servant and huntsman, but rescued by a former Poltimore tenant who overheard two of the trustees arguing and admitting the existence of a rightful heir, and was able to prove the boy's true identity by the presence of an unusual birthmark. He was brought back to Somerset to live at Brympton with the Sydenham family, one of whose daughters he eventually married. Another similar story, but involving twin boys, was told in 1829 by the Revd. Richard Bampfylde, Rector of Poltimore, who then lived at Poltimore House. There was a painting in the house of a man in hunting dress with hawk and hound, named 'Dick the Hunter', an ancestor, and the younger of twin orphaned sons, both of whom were said to have died and been buried at Poltimore. In true fairy-story vein the plot unfolds—wicked trustees, the exhumation of the two little coffins, and the discovery of a skeleton in one and sawdust and stones in the other. To complete the extraordinary tale, the children's nurse was traced who remembered that one twin did indeed have a distinguishing birthmark. Eventually Richard Bampfylde, by this time a young man, was run to ground in Yorkshire, living in a gamekeeper's hut. He came back to his inheritance in 1550 (when he is named as patron of Huxham church) but is said to have lived modestly in a cottage on the estate; could this be the demesne house near the church? Did he live here in the village while he was building what is today the oldest

BELOW
The north east front, 1950s

part of Poltimore House? He is recorded in the parish-muster roll in 1569 as 'Esquire' and a Giles Bampfylde as 'Gentleman', the only two light horsemen in the parish.

Whatever the truth of the kidnapping story, the oldest surviving part, that is the north-west and north-east facing gabled fronts, certainly dates from the second half of the 16th century. Although there is no evidence of this today, it is possible that the early house was more than L-shaped, possibly U-shaped, if not quadrilateral, a view borne out by the 1716 drawing by the topographical artist, Edmund Prideaux, showing a finial on the roofline on the west side matching those on the east front. If the fourth side were also gabled and the courtyard enclosed, the rebuilding of the south front in the early 18th century would have obliterated this part of the Tudor house. The plan would also have been consistent with the size of the

Bampfylde estate and the status of the owner. Being appointed Sheriff of Devon in 1576 it is inconceivable that Richard Bampfylde was not then living in his new house, and that it was of suitable proportions as befitted his rank. He died in 1594, and in his will commends to his son Amyas in quite possessive terms all the hangings, furniture, fittings and bedding 'in my Chamber and Chambers within my howsse of Poltimore there nowe called or knowne by the name or names of the Parlor Chamber the Sollar Chamber the hall Chamber and the Chamber over the Kitchen', thus confirming the existence of a substantial building by this date. Inside, the domestic arrangement was more advanced than what would be expected in the middle of the 16th century, with the kitchens adjacent to the parlour, instead of being at the opposite end of the hall. The staircase wound up through a tower built into the right angle of the L-shaped structure formed by the two gabled wings that remain today. The main entrance was through a wide archway on the north side and this led, to the left, into the great hall of the house (now the Saloon) on the east range. The great hall was not open to the roof, as was still common in large houses in the 16th century, but had a higher ceiling than the adjacent parlour and may have been enriched with decorative plasterwork of the period or heavily moulded beams—all of which was replaced in the mid-18th century by the rococo decoration seen today. Surviving 16th-century features—stone-mullioned windows, original Beerstone chimneypieces and remnants of fine carving—show that the house was of superior construction, advanced design and finished to a very high standard when compared with houses of equivalent status in the South West. Carpenters' marks and other symbols that are often found in English building from the medieval period onwards have been discovered in the roof timbers of the north front. One seal-like mark represents a six-petal symbol, a mark of religious or occult significance, possibly intended to protect the fabric of the house.

How carefully this ground was first surveyed by Richard Bampfylde's builders is not known, but they certainly chose well, if not fortuitously, as the house has never been liable to flooding, whereas the park, grounds and stable block, situated at a lower level and on alluvial soil, have suffered in this respect from time to time. Construction was mostly of local red sandstone with dressings of cream-coloured Beerstone and the occasional use of purple volcanic stone from the neighbourhood in the coigns—in other words perhaps 'a show of polychrome masonry' as was popular in south-west England in the 16th and early 17th centuries. The original roof was of pegged slates from the South Hams, laid in diminishing courses. The whole appearance must have been stunning, and quite different from the bland effect produced by the rendering in stucco, which was done at a later date.

Having failed to oust Richard from his Poltimore estate, the trustees continued to quarrel over the North Molton property. In 1577 there was a suit between St Maur, Zouche and Cantilupe on the one side and Stowell, John Fortescue and Richard Bampfylde on the other. Both Zouche and Cantilupe were landowners in the Midlands and Yorkshire, so may well have been related to two of the 'villainous trustees' involved in the kidnapping, said to have come from the north of England. Their attempts to keep the North Molton lands were finally defeated by Richard's son, Amyas Bampfylde (1551-1625) who inherited the Poltimore and North Molton properties on his father's death in 1594.

Amyas Bampfylde built both Bampfylde House in Exeter and the house on his North Molton estate where he seems mainly to have lived

instead of at Poltimore. In Bampfylde House there was once a massive oak chimneypiece featuring King Charles I mounted on a charger and flanked by the figures of Peace and Plenty with two grotesque statues of a Cavalier and a Puritan on the outsides. Jenkins, in his *History of Exeter*, states that Sir Amyas Bampfylde had placed it there soon after the Restoration. This is incorrect, as Amyas died in 1625, so it is more likely that it was the work of Sir Coplestone Bampfylde, 2nd Baronet, another ardent Royalist, who may also have had the plaster panel with the Stuart arms, together with the letters C R and the date 1666, placed in the house in Poltimore village already mentioned (The Towan House). The chimneypiece was removed from Bampfylde House at some time in the 19th century and until 1921 adorned the main staircase in Poltimore House. It was taken to North Molton by Lord Poltimore in that year, a move which saved it from destruction when Bampfylde House suffered bomb damage in the Exeter air raids of 1942 and was subsequently demolished.

The loss of Bampfylde House meant also the loss of fine plasterwork ceilings very similar

TOP

Staircase at Poltimore House showing the Bampfylde House chimneypiece

BOTTOM

Plaster plaque in a Poltimore cottage dated 1666 with the Royal Arms

to ones at Poltimore. This type of plasterwork in Devon was known in particular from the 16th to the 18th centuries through the work of several generations of the Abbott family of Frithelstock in North Devon. Plasterwork of this quality and decoration by the Abbotts can be seen at Forde House, Newton Abbot (1610) and The Grange, Broadhembury (1603) while Bampfylde House itself is known to have been 'improved' in the early 17th century. In spite of his other interests, therefore, Amyas Bampfylde may have contributed to some of the post-1600 plasterwork decoration at his ancestral house, especially that of the dining room and the rooms above. The design in the former was of double-moulded ribs arranged in geometrical

patterns of squares and decorated with sprays of pomegranates and marigolds or cornflowers. In the centre of the squares were various decorative features, the fleur-de-lys, shells, a cluster of oak leaves and acorns, a dog jumping through leaves after a squirrel, and other animals. In the room above was a simpler ceiling, with double-moulded ribs, here enriched with grape-vine tendrils and sprays of flowers at angles identical to those below. The walls of this room had linenfold panelling but that was removed many years ago; reportedly to a museum in California, although it has never been traced. Sadly, both these fine ceilings were allowed to disintegrate in the 1970s.

Richard Bampfylde is commemorated by a typical Tudor monument in St Mary's church, comprising the recumbent figures of himself and his wife Elizabeth Sydenham. Above the monument lie the fragments of a stone plaque which was originally set over the back door of a row of four village almshouses built in 1631 by Richard's grandson, John Bampfylde, father of John, 1st Baronet. Carved in the stone are the heads of John Bampfylde's wife, Elizabeth Drake, and their son Amyas, both of whom died in 1629, together with four smaller heads, presumably of their remaining children. In memory of his wife

ABOVE

Detail of 17th-century plasterwork in dining room ceiling

RIGHT

*Tomb of Richard
Bampfylde and his
wife in Poltimore
Church*

and son John Bampfylde gave money and land adjoining Poltimore churchyard and in Pinhoe to provide four dwellings and relief for the poor of Poltimore and Huxham. If the two last parishes had no deserving poor, the parishes of Pinhoe and Broadclyst should benefit; furthermore if the revenues were not enough to support those chosen in Huxham, Pinhoe and Broadclyst, these parishes should supply the wherewithal so that Poltimore should not be charged. This charitable deed is commemorated by a charming inscription on the plaque

> Grudge not my laurell
> Rather blesse that bower
> Which made the death of two
> The life of fower.

To return to Richard Bampfylde's building: to judge by an illustration of Poltimore House by Edmund Prideaux, showing a rectangular lake, or canal, which forks and forms a semi-circle either side of the north-

Poltimore in Devon Sr Copleston Bampfyld

east wing, it could once have been a moated hall with gables on all sides. This may be a rough sketch showing the house before c.1680, although Prideaux produced the drawing of the Tudor house with its three gables and wide carriage entrance on the north front in 1716. By 1700, however, the lake had been filled in and underground drains laid which are still used today. This work may have been done around 1681, which is the date on the stone pillars surmounted by balls at the turning in from the Broadclyst road, known and still marked on the Ordnance Survey map as The Bowls (The Bowls have since been re-sited a few yards away from the road, but are still a landmark). Prideaux's later drawing of 1727 shows, with the lake gone, the entirely new south-east front built by Richard's descendant, Sir Coplestone Warwick Bampfylde. Except for mid-19th-century alterations by the 1st Baron Poltimore, the exterior of the house was virtually unchanged from this period until the extensive south-west wing was added in 1908.

ABOVE

The north front of Poltimore House in 1716 as drawn by Edmund Prideaux

12

Royalist to Parliamentarian: Conflict and a Hard-won Treaty

Before the 17th century there are no records of any notable historical events at Poltimore, but with the onset of the Civil War the Bampfyldes and their estate became deeply involved. Richard's grandson, John Bampfylde (1610–1650), son of John and Elizabeth Bampfylde, was a Royalist, and in 1641 made a Baronet by Charles I. At that time most of Devon, including the city of Exeter, was in the hands of the Parliamentary forces, the only two Royalist garrisons in the Exeter area being the fortified house of Sir John Acland nearby at Columb John, and Poltimore House. John Bampfylde supported a detachment of troops from Poltimore to raid Exeter and maintain a stronghold in Sidwell Street, a continual thorn in the side of the Parliamentary garrison until the city surrendered to the Royalists in September 1643. But, as in all civil conflicts there were divided loyalties; nor were 17th-century Devon landowners above switching their allegiances. In fact, John Bampfylde's royalism did not last long, and in 1642, much to the displeasure of the King, he became 'a zealous partisan of the Parliament'. Rather surprisingly, after this volte face, Prince Maurice, younger brother of the celebrated Royalist general, Prince Rupert, who took the city for the King, granted a free pardon to John Bampfylde and several other Devon notables.

Among those who changed sides were Sir John Northcote from Upton Pyne on the other side of the Exe, and Sir Samuel Rolle. In 1642, Bampfylde, Northcote & Rolle between them raised a force of 8000 tenants and farm workers armed, somewhat primitively, with

OPPOSITE
In the woodland

scythes and pitchforks, 'flayles, clubs, halberts and such like rusticke weapons'. With this 17th-century 'Dad's Army' John Bampfylde proceeded to Plymouth (throughout the war a Parliamentary stronghold) and was installed as commander of the Fort. But by the summer of 1645 he was back at Poltimore, with prisoners—whom he is said to have kept chained in the cellars—to join the victorious Sir Thomas Fairfax, fresh from defeating the King at the Battle of Naseby.

It must have seemed to the people of Devon in that turbulent year of 1645 that Fairfax was everywhere at once. He was Commander-in-Chief of the New Model Army, Cromwell being his Lieutenant General of Horse. Large parts of Devon were still under the Royalists, and on his way west Fairfax diverted to Bridgwater to take the castle. Here an incident occurred that nearly changed the course of history. The wife of Colonel Wyndham, commander of the castle, was so incensed at the arrival not only of Cromwell, but of Fairfax himself, on the banks of the River Parrett opposite the castle, that she seized a musket and rushed to the ramparts. Baring one breast, in Amazonian fashion, she took a pot shot at the two Generals but succeeded only in hitting a sergeant. Bridgwater fell to the Parliamentary forces and Cromwell turned back towards Gloucester. Fairfax continued south and captured Tiverton, made his headquarters at Ottery St Mary and placed garrisons at

ABOVE

The Saloon, formerly the Great Hall where the treaty was negotiated

Topsham, Crediton and Stoke Canon and with John Bampfylde at Poltimore House. From Ottery he pushed on across the River Exe, retook Dartmouth and then dashed into north Devon, defeating the Royalists in a never-to-be-forgotten battle at Great Torrington.

After his victory at Torrington Fairfax galloped across the county to Exeter, then besieged by the Parliamentarians, and on arrival sent in a message to the Governor, Sir John Berkeley, inviting him to surrender in order to save the city from further bloodshed. Berkeley finally gave in and agreed to meet Fairfax, and in April 1646 asked for safe conduct for four of his nominees and six of his officers. The meeting place was to be Poltimore House; the men chosen were Robert Walker, a former Mayor and MP for the city, Thomas Knott, Thomas Kendall and Thomas Ford. General Fairfax, however, wanted six on each side and wrote to Berkeley: 'I agree the time Friday next, the place Poultimore [sic] House; the Commissioners on my part: Thomas Hammond, Lieutenant Generall of the Ordinance, Col. Sir Hardress Waller, Col. Lambert, Col. Edward Harley, Col. Fry and Commissary Stane.' As it turned out only Robert Walker and Thomas Knott from the Royalist side rode out from the city with Sir John Berkeley and his officers, Sir Henry Berkeley, Sir George Parry, Colonel Ashburnham, Colonel Godolphin and Captain FitzGerald. (A John Weare may also have been of the party.)

It is tempting to try and imagine the scene at Poltimore when the little band of King's men from Exeter with their swords and plumed hats dismounted from their horses and entered the great hall of the house to begin the lengthy discussions. Sir John Bampfylde and his wife, Gertrude Coplestone, had already received General Fairfax as their guest and now they were to play host to the enemy. The main hall on the north-east side of the house, the present Saloon, where the Treaty is thought to have been negotiated, would still have had its Elizabethan wainscotting and large chimneypiece. From the hall led the winding Tudor staircase to the bell tower and the barely furnished first-floor rooms under the gables where the men from the two sides would have kept their distances. The proceedings in the hall, we are told, continued from Friday, 3rd April,1646 until the following Wednesday, every day and for most of the night until all objections were resolved. Much wax and tallow would have been burnt and undoubtedly a great deal of sack or wine drunk, brought

up from the cellars where John Bampfylde is said to have kept the prisoners he took at Plymouth. Outside in the park the troopers escorting the negotiators were camped, both men of Cromwell's New Model Army and the soldiers accompanying Sir John Berkeley from Exeter, their horses tethered under the trees. Three hundred years after the event a dozen or more nine-inch iron nails of the Commonwealth period were discovered hammered in at an angle—presumably for use as tethering posts—at the base of an oak tree when it was brought down in a gale. At the time of the Civil War the village of Poltimore consisted of cottages (some still standing) of stone, cob and thatch with smithy and grain stores, all clustered near the ancient church—dwellings of great simplicity compared with the panelled splendour of the Tudor house of the Bampfyldes. No doubt gossip and rumour enlivened the village during the six days of confabulations going on in the big house across the park.

Finally, on Thursday, 9th April, 1646 the deliberations ended. The Treaty of Exeter was signed by Fairfax, either at Poltimore House, or possibly at the Acland's house at Columb John, a mile or more away, while the documents on behalf of the King were witnessed in Exeter. Fairfax, now joined by Cromwell, had briefly made their headquarters at Columb John, where it seems that the Aclands had been won over by the good behaviour of the Parliamentary troops. Lady Acland wrote to Cromwell, 'I received such ample testimony of your love when you were pleased to quarter at my house as I cannot sufficiently express my thankfulness for the same.' Perhaps the nearness of Columb John to Poltimore was the reason for choosing the latter as the meeting place for the two sides to negotiate the Treaty. Cromwell himself probably did not come to Poltimore, but is said to have quartered troops near Thorverton and, however polite they had been at Columb John, they certainly set about damaging elements of Silverton church.

There is no way of knowing if John Bampfylde was party to the negotiations at Poltimore House, but his uncle, Thomas Bampfylde, a leading Presbyterian and strong supporter of Cromwell, was probably in the house at the time, and both may have been present at the signing of the Treaty. Fairfax, the tough dealer, got his way, although to the King's people the terms looked good at first. There were 23 clauses in the agreement, the first being that the city and garrison of Exeter, together with the Castle and other places of

defence with ammunition, arms, provisions and 'the furniture of war belonging to the Garrison' was to be made over to General Fairfax on the following Monday, 13th April at 12 noon (except for those in the St Thomas' Ward of the city and Mount Radford, which had to be delivered by 6 pm on 7th April.) It was rather a tall order given the short time, and it was only afterwards that they realised they had been duped. However, the Treaty effectively ended civil strife in Devon and Cornwall—Pendennis Castle at Falmouth having already fallen. Ten days later Dunster Castle in Somerset, which had been besieged by the Parliamentarians for six months, surrendered to the forces of Sir Thomas Fairfax. In the South West the war was over and Poltimore's historic role had been established.

John Bampfylde died in 1650 and was succeeded by the eldest of his sons out of nineteen children. The 2nd Baronet, named Coplestone after his mother's family of Coplestone near Crediton and Warleigh near Plymouth, was a very different character from his Puritanical father. Born in 1636, he was only fourteen when he inherited the Poltimore estates, described by John Prince in *The Worthies of Devon* as 'the gentile well accommodated seat of Poltimore House, which stands in the middle of the parish, whose manor comprizeth the whole, unto which belongeth a park, warren, dove cote, ponds &c. all fitted for hospitality; upon the account whereof, and its zeal in religion this family has been very eminent.' Coplestone Bampfylde certainly had money to spend from his inheritances—from his mother's estate as well as Poltimore and North Molton, and he spent it, living very much as a grand seigneur, travelling about the country with a splendid retinue and distributing gifts. He became a member of an underground Royalist movement, had to go into hiding and at one time was imprisoned in the Tower of London.

After the Restoration of Charles II in 1660 Sir Coplestone was able publicly to declare his royalist colours. In 1937 the textiles collection of The Art Institute of Chicago acquired from a resident of New York a 17th-century Honiton-lace sash now believed to have been made for Sir Coplestone Bampfylde on his appointment as High

Sheriff of Devon in 1661. Worked into the lace are the initials CB, with the words Baronet, Vive le Roy, Carolus Rex and the date 1661, together with symbols of the Restoration such as Tudor roses, oak leaves, acorns and Prince of Wales's feathers. It has been suggested that the CB refers to Charles's Queen, the date 1661 being when Charles II married Catherine of Braganza, but this is probably just a coincidence. Coplestone Bampfylde was one of only two baronets in England at that period with the initials CB, the other being a Sussex landowner, while the proximity of Honiton, the famous Devon lace-making town, to Poltimore, points to a local place of origin. The importation of foreign lace was banned at that time and anyone doing so was liable to a heavy fine, so Coplestone Bampfylde had good reason to commission his lace from makers only a few miles from his home.

Since Richard Bampfylde's day there had been no important alterations to the late-16th-century house. As we have seen, Richard's son, Amyas, added some internal decorations, but was more interested in his north Devon property, and two successive generations had made no additions as far as can be seen. The period of the Civil War was in any case not conducive to country-house building. It thus fell to Sir Coplestone Bampfylde, the second of that name, with his money and flair to embark on the next phase of development.

The Bampfylde Builders: from the 17th to the 20th Century

Coplestone Bampfylde, 2nd Baronet (1636–91) carried out an extensive modernisation of his father's Tudor house during the period 1680–90. Although the layout remained more or less the same, the original winding stair in the tower was replaced by a new oak staircase, typically late-17th-century with square newel posts, turned pendants and finials and turned balusters with a flat, moulded handrail. The windows were probably altered at the same time, all this work being consistent with the date of 1681 of the 'Bowls' on the gate piers marking the entrance to the estate from the Broadclyst road. At one time it was thought that Coplestone was also responsible for the richly decorated Saloon, formerly the hall of the house where the Treaty of Exeter had been signed in 1646, and that it had been designed in honour of the future Queen Anne who, tradition says, may have visited Poltimore during her tour of the South West after the Restoration. The decoration includes plaster heads said to be of George, Prince of Denmark, Anne's consort, and of their only child to survive infancy, William, Duke of Gloucester, identified by his abnormally large head (he died of hydrocephalus in 1700). However, this would date the fine plasterwork to the end of the 17th century, whereas rococo work of this quality was not known in the South West for at least another thirty or forty years. Sir Coplestone Bampfylde died in 1691 at about the same time as his son Hugh, leaving a two-year-old heir to the baronetcy—his grandson, Coplestone Warwick Bampfylde.

It might seem, therefore, that the second Sir Coplestone (1689–

1727) was the architect of this major embellishment; however, in view of his somewhat short life it seems more likely to have been his son Richard Warwick Bampfylde, 4th Baronet. (The confusion between the two Coplestone Bampfyldes, 2nd and 3rd Baronets, whose lives both spanned the last years of the 17th century is understandable, and is confounded by the fact that Coplestone Warwick Bampfylde's brother, John Bampfylde, named his son by Margaret Warre of Hestercombe in Somerset, Coplestone Warre Bampfylde. It was Coplestone Warre Bampfylde, an artist, who created the Secret Garden at Hestercombe, near Taunton, which was rediscovered and restored in the 1990s. Nevertheless, the royal connection with Poltimore House is enhanced by the fact that Queen Anne presented Coplestone Warwick Bampfylde with a portrait of herself by Sir Godfrey Kneller which, however, could not have been painted until after her accession in 1702 as it shows the Queen in state robes with orb and sceptre. This painting hung in the house, although probably not in the Saloon, until the sale of the contents in 1923; its whereabouts is not now known, although a copy is believed to exist in Washington DC. A three-quarter-length portrait of Coplestone Warwick Bampfylde, by an unknown artist, shows him wearing a full-skirted coat of apricot-coloured velvet and lace cravat, standing with hand on hip, a pose typical of the period. His wife, Gertrude Carew, in steel-blue satin, provides a complementary painting of the same size; both can be seen at Hartland Abbey in North Devon.

Whoever its creator, the exuberantly decorated and gilded 18th-century Saloon has been described as 'one of the finest rooms of its kind in the county' by Cherry and Pevsner. Poltimore could not, of course, rival in magnificence the great houses of the mid-18th century such as those Palladian masterpieces Chiswick House or Holkham

Hall in Norfolk, and no doubt was not intended to. Nevertheless, the cornice in the Saloon is classical in design, the outer walls draped with swags of fruit, foliage and flowers in plaster with oval mirrors in carved and gilded lime wood frames. The chimneypiece was rebuilt in the centre of the inner wall with a fire surround in white-veined marble with massive ormolu-gilt swags of fruit, steel grate and mantelpiece of painted wood and carved with a hound's head and hunting horns and hounds' tails on either side. Over the chimneypiece there was once a carved frame with broken pediment containing a small statuary group, the frame surrounding an oil painting of the coast of North Devon or Cornwall. Above the mahogany doors at the ends of the room are lion masks with elaborate swags of fruit and flowers and on either side of the doors, tall alcoves, which until 1920 contained statues of biblical subjects, one of St John as a child and the other the Son of the Shunamite (the subject of one of the Prophet Elisha's miracles, 2 Kings, 4.xii). The plaster ceiling features what is thought to be the head of Queen Anne (although Apollo has also been suggested as a subject) surrounded by floating clouds with sunrays radiating outwards through a laurel wreath towards two pairs of storks, the rest of the ceiling ornamented with swirling ropes and seaweed ending in shells at the four corners. When newly finished and

lit by many candles the whole effect must have been extraordinary.

If the second Sir Coplestone was not responsible for this splendid creation he certainly carried out other transformations. He constructed the courtyard plan and the south front, as seen in Edmund Prideaux's drawing of 1727 with Sir Coplestone's name inscribed. It should be mentioned that Edmund Prideaux made only two journeys to the South West of England, in 1716 and 1727. His one drawing of 1716, made for the 3rd Baronet, shows the Tudor north range of Poltimore House and in front of it a wide canal flanked by clipped trees and grassy rides, leading straight to the house and dividing to form branches on either side of the house. This appears to be a canal after the style of the Hampton Court water courses made fashionable in the mid-17th century, here a landscape feature as well as a fishpond, witness the two figures fishing in the left-hand corner of the drawing. Future archaeological investigations might throw light on the existence of such a watercourse. The fact that it was drawn in 1716 does not preclude the possibility that the canal had been introduced by the first Sir Coplestone in the mid-17th century.

Sir Coplestone Warwick Bampfylde, however, undoubtedly redesigned the gardens on the north front during the eleven years between 1716 and 1727. When Edmund Prideaux again visited Poltimore in 1727 he drew a different view of the north front, this time ascribed to Sir Richard Bampfylde, the 3rd baronet's son who must only just have inherited the estate in that year. The canal had been filled in and a garden laid out with serpentine paths, statues and topiary— occupying approximately the lawned area on the east side of the house today. Sir Coplestone certainly had money to spend, for by 1727 the entirely new south range of Poltimore House had been built, viewed at the end of an avenue of trees and complete with grand symmetrical eleven-bay front, central entrance and dormer windows alternately rounded and pointed, in the roof. The deer park was probably enlarged at this stage and the forecourt in front of the house fenced off.

The new south front contrasts vividly with the Elizabethan north elevation of the house. Prideaux's drawing shows that it was symmetrical about the central doorway which is contained in a discreetly projecting bay three windows wide, flanked on either side by equal lengths of wall each containing four windows on each storey. The house is now plastered externally with its only decoration being

banded pilasters flanking the central bay and at each corner. Instead of presenting a row of gables, the roof is tucked behind a panelled parapet. The whole effect is one of restraint, something that is not generally characteristic of this period of architecture in England when grand buildings were often built with a lavish use of classical motifs. Indeed it gives the appearance much more of a French mansion of this period than of an English one, and one wonders if Sir Coplestone Bampfylde, if he had not actually been to France, for which there is no evidence, might have visited and been influenced by houses in England designed in a French style or by French architects, such as Petworth house in Sussex c.1686 or Dyrham Park in Gloucestershire c.1692.

A century later Ackermann's print of 1827, the fourth of the images of Poltimore House known to exist before photography, is of the stuccoed south-east front with fallow deer (*Cervus dama*), a species of European origin, free to graze right up to the house, a practice which continued until 1939. Saxton's map of Devonshire engraved in 1575 shows Poltimore as a deer park, probably spread over many acres where the deer would have been hunted. By the 18th century, when deer were considered as much ornament as quarry, the enclosure would have been brought to the vicinity of the house, and the herd, when necessary, culled for venison. In the late 19th century, when the park was enlarged, the fallow-deer

ABOVE

The south front of Poltimore House in 1827

26

herd was augmented by Japanese Sika deer (*Cervus nippon*), a smaller breed with attractively marked heads. In the 20th century Lord Poltimore also kept black Welsh Mountain sheep in the park, the descendants of which are today at Hartland Abbey in North Devon.

During the hundred years from the middle of the 18th century the Bampfyldes, having greatly embellished their grand house, became involved in politics, and the 3rd, 4th and 5th Baronets successively sat as first Tory and then Whig MPs for Exeter or Devon. No carpet-baggers moving around the country pocketing boroughs, they lived in their constituencies either at Poltimore House or in Exeter at Bampfylde House. The most enthusiastic of the Poltimore politicians was Sir Charles Warwick Bampfylde, 5th Baronet, who was elected to represent Exeter eight times between 1774 and 1807. In 1776, the year he succeeded to the baronetcy, he married Catherine Moore (1754–1832), whose full-length portrait by Sir Joshua Reynolds, himself a Devonian, hung in Poltimore House until after 1885 and is now in the Tate. It is a striking example of portraiture of that period, indicating the influence of the great Dutch masters on Reynolds's style. Lady Bampfylde is painted in a baroque landscape, which could easily be part of Poltimore's wooded grounds before the 19th-century pinetum was made, and it is not difficult to imagine her entertaining her husband's political cronies in Poltimore's white and gold Saloon. Music was surely also performed in this fine room; from the 1740s onwards the Bampfyldes are recorded as subscribers to new musical compositions (cantatas, anthems and sonatas), Catherine Bampfylde in 1784 contributing to Edward Jones's *Musical and Poetical Relicks of the Welsh Bards*. Thomas Hudson's painting of the same Catherine Bampfylde, in many ways a more arresting portrait, is now at Hartland Abbey in North Devon. She is without the powdered headdress of the Reynolds portrait, dressed in pale satin, unadorned, with a posy in one hand.

In 1779 Reynolds also painted the 5th Baronet's brother, John Codrington Warwick Bampfylde, in a double portrait, also in the Tate, with his friend George Huddesford. The two young men could not have been more different in both appearance and character. Huddesford the elegant wit and satirist who later became a cleric, regards the artist with a sideways glance and a hint of a smile; Bampfylde, an aspiring poet and musician, serious-faced, less confident, casually and romantically dressed and holding some sort of musical instrument, accepting a printed paper from his friend. Bampfylde lived modestly at Catshole on the River Teign near Chudleigh, making occasional forays to Exeter where he is said to have played on the Cathedral organ. The organist William Jackson (1730-1803) an Exeter musician of merit, was also a popular composer of ballads, many of which were set to lines written by John Bampfylde. Another admirer of Bampfylde was the poet Robert Southey who may well have been the observer of his poor young contemporary as being 'craz'd with care or coss'd in hapless love', a state of affairs which continued until 1778 when, on arrival in London he fell in love with Reynolds's niece, Mary Palmer. This affection was either not reciprocated, or else it was stopped from getting anywhere by Sir Joshua himself. John Bampfylde dedicated his Sixteen Sonnets to his love and, when he was rejected, wrote his 'Stanzas to a Lady' expressing his despair:

'In vain from clime to clime I stray
To chase thy beauteous form away,
And banish every care;
In vain to quit thy charms I try
Since every thought creates a sigh,
And every wish a tear.'

ABOVE

*George Huddesford (L)
and John Codrington
Bampfylde. A double
portrait by Sir Joshua
Reynolds, 1779. ©Tate,
London, 2005*

Reynolds had Bampfylde more or less thrown out of his house in Leicester Fields, St Martins-in-the-Fields (presumably after completing the double portrait), and as a result Bampfylde, leaving in a fit of rage, broke some of the windows. For this he was arrested and fined £20—paid by his friends Huddesford and Joseph Millidge, the publisher of his verses. After this episode he became insane and died of consumption in about 1796. Much of Bampfylde's poetry is at times almost Tennysonian in its melancholy—the despair, the dripping eaves and lost hopes, as these lines from A 'Wet Summer' illustrate:

'All ye who far from town in rural hall,
Like me were wont to dwell near pleasant field,
Enjoying all the sunny day did yield —
With me the change lament, in irksome thrall,
By rains incessant held; for now no call
From early swain invites my hand to wield
The scythe. In parlour dim I sit concealed,
And mark the lessening sand from hour-glass fall;
Or, neath my window view the wistful train
Of dripping poultry, whom the vine's broad leaves
Shelter no more. Mute is the mournful plain,
Silent the swallow sits beneath the thatch,
And vacant hind hangs pensive o'er his hatch,
Counting the frequent drip from reeded eaves.'

Aside from politics, John Codrington Bampfylde's brother Charles seems also to have been interested in music and the arts; he even had 'Ballads, Catches, Glees and Part songs' dedicated to him and which were sung at the Pic-Nics (assembly rooms) in Bath. He subscribed to The New Musical Fund established in 1786 for the relief of 'Decayed Musicians, their Widows and Orphans'. He also commissioned paintings—presumably the one of his wife by Reynolds—and one of his favourite hunter by George Stubbs which, it is recorded, never left the artist's studio. On one occasion the artist Thomas Jones was much put out when Sir Charles 'bespoke a picture at 30 guineas. This I finished in July (1775) and sent home, but a few days afterward I heard it was sold with the rest of his furniture—whereby I lost not only my picture but the frame also...!'

Charles Bampfylde fared little better than his brother towards the end of his life; he was murdered by his housekeeper's husband, and with him ended the long tenure of political posts. His heir, George Warwick Bampfylde, 6th Baronet, declined to stand for Parliament for Exeter on the grounds that the process had cost his father more than £80,000. Westminster connections continued,

ABOVE

George Warwick Bampfylde, 1st Baron Poltimore. Photograph Dick Brownridge

however, when William IV used his prerogative of creating peers to carry the Great Reform Bill of 1832 through the House of Lords, and George Warwick Bampfylde was made 1st Baron Poltimore.

On his elevation to the peerage in 1831, Lord Poltimore embarked on the third great period of rebuilding and renovation undertaken by the Bampfyldes at their ancestral mansion. To begin with, he built the impressive staircase with its handsome iron balustrade, rising from the hall floor of stone inset with black marble squares, and seen through four Ionic columns which support the friezes round the hall. These columns mark the limit of the south range built by Sir Coplestone Warwick Bampfylde in the 18th century. Similar columns with more ornate friezes in the Corinthian style are at the top of the stone staircase. The main, rather heavy, porch was also added after 1831, its iron gates incorporating the letter P in the centre surmounted by a baron's coronet. A projecting, round single-storey bay window was added to the west end of the library and a single-storey extension to the dining room on the east side, while various service buildings were put up on the north side of the house. The interior decoration of the Red Drawing Room and the Library may also date from this period. The former is the largest room in the pre-1908 house, having at the west end two fluted columns and pilasters with elaborate composite capitals supporting a neo-classical plasterwork ceiling. The walls were covered with red silk panels, whence the room gets its name and, until

ABOVE

The entrance hall in
1920

31

vandalized in the 1990s, a Carrara marble chimneypiece adorned the east range. Another theory regarding the dating of this room is that the architect James Johnson, who had rebuilt Killerton House for Sir John Dyke Acland and worked on Sir Charles Bampfylde's house in London, may have had a hand in it, which would put it into the late 18th century.

The design of the Library on the west side of the south front was more restrained, the columns plain with Corinthian capitals and the fire surround of white marble. In the late 19th century the walls were papered with a pattern of exotic green pheasants in foliage. When the paper was removed during the hospital era the names of the paperhangers were discovered underneath with a date in the 1880s. A paper of similar style featuring green parrots was used in one of the principal bedrooms on the floor above. A late-19th-century photograph of the Library shows it fitted with tall bookcases, while the Red Drawing Room and Saloon were both richly furnished as reception rooms. The Bampfylde family paintings already mentioned,

together with others that were sold at the 1923 sale of contents, were hung in all these rooms and on the imperial staircase.

Outside in the grounds on the north side of the house, the 19th century saw the planting of many specimens of rare ornamental and forest trees. Among earlier plantings were the two impressive lime avenues behind the house, the one leading from the house to the church probably dating from the time of the accession of George I in 1714, and still a fine sight in spring with its carpet of primroses and bluebells. The average height of these lime trees is 120 feet, although one or two exceed this by at least 15 feet. The other, western, avenue which may not have been planted at the same time, was felled in 1956, to the dismay of many people, and replanted with poplars which now, as mature trees, are a graceful addition to this part of the landscape. Behind the lines of

BELOW
The Library in about 1912

poplars the felled lime trunks have over the last forty years regenerated to make a new avenue. According to the 1801 Ordnance Survey map of Devon, on which the Poltimore church-to-house lime avenue is marked, the land west of the avenue was enclosed as fields, including the area depicted by Prideaux a century before as formal grounds. Sir George Bampfylde's enoblement in 1831 may have triggered the decision to develop these acres as pleasure grounds. A few years later, by 1835, the parish road which passed close to the house was moved further to the east, thus extending the deer park and removing the everyday traffic of the village from the 1st Baron's private territory.

The arboretum behind the house was begun in about 1840 by James Veitch, son of the Scottish gardener John Veitch, who came to the South West from Scotland at the end of the 18th century and whose family gained a reputation for introducing plants new to Europe from Chile, China, Java and North America. John Veitch carried out a great deal of new planting at Killerton House, only two miles away, and eventually established a nursery at Budlake near Broadclyst on land

ABOVE
The lime avenue

given to him by Sir Thomas Dyke Acland of Killerton. At one time he rented ground in Poltimore parish (at Bamberrys, or Bamberries) for his plants, and undoubtedly the work done at Killerton presented his son with the opportunity to lay out the Poltimore arboretum. Quite large trees would be brought from outside, often from London Docks by coastal smacks to the small quays at Topsham and hauled to their destination by horse drawn wagons. Some of the very first seedlings of *Sequoiadendron giganteum*, commonly known as Wellingtonia, were brought to England from California by the Victorian plant collector William Lobb in about 1853 and planted in the Poltimore pinetum. Five of these huge trees survive today, one more than 137 feet high with a spread of 22 feet, and all of them, as well as the Coast Redwood (*Sequoia sempervirens*), are over 105 feet high. Other especially interesting trees are: the Caucasian Firs (*Abies nordmanniana*) of which there were five; the Colorado Douglas Firs (*Pseudotsuga glauca*); the Cork Oak (*Quercus suber*) said to have been planted by Sir Walter Raleigh (unlikely, as this species was not introduced into England until the end of the 17th century); the Japanese Umbrella Pine (*Sciadopitys verticillata*), one of the five sacred trees of Japan and extensively planted in temple gardens; the Lucombe Oak (*Quercus hispanica Lucombeana*), a hybrid between a Turkey Oak and a Cork Oak first raised by the Exeter nurseryman Lucombe in 1765, of which there are a number; the Purple Beech (*Fagus sylvatica purpurea*) a magnificent specimen over

LEFT
Japanese cedar and Monkey Puzzle

110 feet high; Schrenk's Spruce (*Picea schrenkiana*) and the aptly named Tiger-tailed Spruce (*Picea polita*); the Silver Maple (*Acer saccharinum*) and the Sweet Gum (*Liquidambar styraciflua*). There are also some beautiful cedars (*Cedrus libani*, *deodara* and *atlantica* and two specimens of Western Yellow Cedar (*Thuja plicata*), one of which has been layered to provide a great branched trunk from the ground. Originally there were nine Monkey Puzzles (*Araucaria auraucana*), probably late-19th-century plantings, in a group around the lawns near the house. Only a few now remain, although seedlings have recently grown.

This wonderful collection should now be a perpetual reserve for plant and bird life; for, besides much else, many kinds of orchid abound, including (rarely) Autumn Ladies Tresses (*Orchis spiranthes spiranthes*), and there have been seen or heard in past times herons, kingfishers, lapwings, nightjars, woodpeckers, goldcrests, buzzards, peregrines, owls and even the nightingale. In 1957 the botanist Maynard Greville carried out a survey of the arboretum and

ABOVE

The arboretum looking north from the house

measured many of the trees. Bats, probably pipistrelles, have always roosted in the house and, in the 1950s at least, the ceiling of the Red Drawing Room was their favoured haunt on summer nights.

Through these woodlands, parallel with and between the two avenues, a wide grassy track led to the house and gave a fine view of the gabled front. (It is hereabouts that one of Poltimore's ghosts is said to haunt—the Red Lady, wringing her hands over some tragic event or other). A granite obelisk that has lain for over a century in separate blocks in the grounds may have been intended either for the end of this central path, or for the top of the western lime avenue. Two huge stone chairs, sited one on each side, and known in later days as 'Lord and Lady Poltimore' also once graced the top of the avenue, but unfortunately disappeared in the 1970s. This part of the original arboretum is now under separate ownership.

The granite of the obelisk, a pinkish/grey speckled stone with pieces of feldspar or crystalline mineral in it, probably came from the Blackingstone quarries near Moretonhampstead on the east side of Dartmoor. The huge blocks would have been brought on wagons drawn by teams of heavy horses the distance of nearly twenty miles from the quarry to Poltimore, and must have provided a rare sight being drawn slowly through the narrow lanes and finally into the entrance to the woodlands near the walled garden. Today these great blocks lie in a circle within a clearing, forgotten and mysterious. However, when some of the stone, not apparently part of the obelisk, was removed in July 2000 to use for new entrance signs to Poltimore village, the initials S L (possibly those of the stonecutter) were found inscribed with the date 1858—the year that Augustus Frederick Bampfylde, Lord Poltimore's son and heir, celebrated his 21st birthday. It can only be speculation that the obelisk was intended to mark this date—

which was a great occasion at Poltimore House for family, friends and tenants. The jollifications, which went on for five days and astonished the county, are colourfully described by the late Eleanor Kerr of Poltimore in her book

BELOW
Part of the 1858 obelisk lying in the arboretum in 2005. Photograph Keith Weedon

Hunting Parson: The Life and Times of the Reverend John Russell. Russell was a great friend of the Bampfylde family, and is portrayed in a panoramic painting by William Widgery, mounted on a grey horse and following the 2nd Baron at the head of the Poltimore Hunt as they gallop towards Huxham Brake below Stoke Hill. On this huge canvas, which used to hang in Poltimore House, the settlements scattered through the landscape from the conical hill of Cadbury Castle on the left, across the Vale of Honiton south to Sidmouth Gap, are recognisable by their clusters of houses and church towers. Russell attended the birthday event at Poltimore in 1858 for which Sir Thomas Acland lent seven cannon from Killerton for the celebratory salvoes. Bands played, fireworks were let off and sports were held in the park. A few days later the whole party moved up to North Molton for a second celebration, where the Reverend Russell opened the ball with Lady Poltimore while Augustus took a local North Molton girl as his partner. The 1st Baron died the same year; was his death the reason why the obelisk was not erected? If it were meant for a celebration perhaps it was felt inappropriate to erect it in the wake of a bereavement. Augustus was already married to Florence Sheridan, a descendant of the playwright and politician Richard Brinsley Sheridan. She was a lady of considerable character, as will be seen, and the instigator of

ABOVE

The walled garden showing the peach houses

many innovations that took place at Poltimore in the next half century.

At the far end of the grounds and overlooked from the churchyard was the walled kitchen garden of seven acres. Completed by 1841, it boasted peach houses, heated glasshouses and a vinery. There were also aviaries at the end of the western lime avenue near the house, where white pheasants and white peacocks and cranes were kept, an exotic spectacle as they picked their way amongst the trees and drank from bowls of turquoise mosaic which were sunk into the ground (and survive today). Lord Poltimore had a great liking for white animals, and as well as the birds, white rabbits and even white deer were part of his menagerie. Another extravaganza of the time was the Chinese Garden, which could be seen from the west windows of the house. There may have been an ornamental water garden here from at least 1801; the OS map shows a quite large enclosed area with, possibly, water on the west side of the house. By the latter part of the century the leat which flowed into the River Clyst had been dammed to form a pool and the garden laid out according to the design of a

BELOW
The Poltimore Hunt crossing Huxham Brake by William Widgery, 1860. Photograph Dick Brownridge

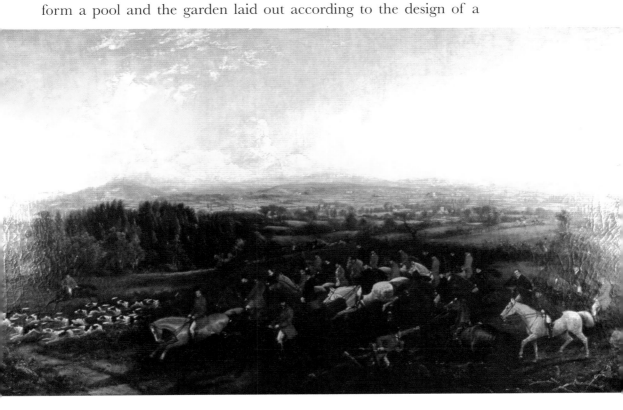

willow-pattern plate, complete with pagoda, bridge and fencing. This stream, which crossed the park and was bridged in two or three places, watered the large herd of fallow deer; in 1892 these numbered 150, although ten years earlier 300 had been recorded. Nearly all traces of the Chinese Garden have now disappeared, but the 1912 photograph gives some idea of its romantic charm, even when overgrown in later years, brightened in summer by the showy yellow flowers with dark centres and huge heart-shaped leaves of *Buphthalmum speciosum*.

Half hidden by two magnificent trees (a Lucombe and a Turkey Oak) behind the north-west side of the house, were the 19th-century stables with clock tower and cupola over the arched entrance. The clock face was a dummy, and the turret empty, because the bell in the tower of the house was considered a good enough alarm and time keeper. Unfortunately this attractive architectural feature was demolished in the 1970s. To the left of the entrance is another fine oak, planted to commemorate the birth in 1859 of Coplestone Richard George Warwick Bampfylde, later 3rd Baron. The tree's girth is circled by a coronet of iron with gilded points that, one hundred and fifty years on,

RIGHT
*The Chinese Garden in
1912*

is inextricable from the trunk; you could say it has entered the heart, if not the soul, of the tree.

The stables and carriage houses, of brick, were arranged on the four sides of the yard with a covered verandah all round under which the carriage horses and hunters could be exercised in wet weather. The coachman lived in the north-east corner of the stable yard, while the grooms, and the strappers and belters looking after the carriages and harness, had to doss down in the haylofts above. Herbert Franklin, who was still living in Poltimore village in the 1950s, remembered these quarters when he started work there as a stable boy in the 1880s, and could look back to 1902 when, as a young groom, he accompanied Lord Poltimore's coach and horses by train from Exeter to London for the Coronation of King Edward VII. The Bampfyldes' London house was at 8 Belgrave Square, although 18th-century Bampfyldes are said to have had a town residence at 38 Grosvenor Square (now the Indonesian Embassy), which had work done on it by John Johnson, the Leicester architect who in 1778–79 rebuilt Killerton House for Sir John Acland. Sir Charles Bampfylde, father of the 1st Baron, also occupied 63 New Cavendish Street in the West End.

Poltimore by the mid-Victorian age had thus become a very large country estate, giving employment to many men outdoors in the gardens, stables and on the estate as a whole, and countless indoor staff as well. On inheriting in 1858, Lord and Lady Poltimore turned

ABOVE

Augustus Frederick Warwick Bampfylde, 2nd Baron Poltimore. Drawing by Frederick Sargent, c. 1890. Reproduced by courtesy of the National Portrait Gallery

RIGHT
Lady (Florence)
Poltimore in coronation
robes 1902

41

their attention to improvements in Poltimore village. Lady Poltimore built, or perhaps rebuilt, the village school in 1861 (she had supported the building of a National School at North Molton at about the same time) and the group of model cottages opposite the church in 1897. There were conditions to this munificence, however. The lawns and flower beds in front of the cottages had to be kept trim and would be visited by Lady Poltimore each Saturday, if she was at home. The children of the village were left in no doubt who ruled the roost at Poltimore; Netta Holmes, daughter of the estate carpenter, recalled being whipped for not curtseying as Lady Poltimore drove through the village! At Christmas, girls attending the school were fitted out with red cloaks and bonnets, and the female staff at the mansion with blue. On Sunday mornings there would be a procession from the house up the avenue of lime trees to the church, Lord Poltimore in front followed by the men on the staff in top hats and the women in their blue cloaks and bonnets. The line of the avenue leads directly towards

BELOW
The indoor staff at Poltimore House c. 1900

ABOVE
Florence Sheridan, wife
of Augustus Bampfylde,
2nd Baron Poltimore.
Photograph Dick
Brownridge

the south transept of the church, where there is a door by which the family entered and assumed their places in the gallery pew overhead, complete with fireplace (nowadays used as the church vestry and organ loft). Thus Lord and Lady Poltimore could view their employees and tenants sitting below—women under the gallery and men in the north transept—and note who was absent. Delinquents may well have had a carpetting the next morning! There is little recorded of the relationship between Lord Poltimore and his tenantry and staff; a group photograph taken just prior to 1914 indicates benevolence on Lord Poltimore's side although, according to the mores of the day, respect and deference were given and expected. One insight into how the Bampfylde family were regarded in the early 20th century comes from a remark written on a postcard by one of the gardeners who was present at Lady Poltimore's funeral in 1909 and responsible for the decoration of the grave, 'Mr Harry [Bampfylde] was terribly cut up...he was the only real mourner and was always with his mother until her death.... he is such a nice toff to talk to.....'

The next enlargement and modernisation of the house took place in 1908. New brick-built kitchens were added at the rear, together with the necessary sculleries, larders, pantries, a laundry and rooms for the staff, and an office for Charles Wreford, the clerk of works. At least 110 workers were employed. Electric light was installed by Whippell & Rowe of Exeter, generated from batteries driven by two 25-hp Ruston Hornsby engines in the stables, and this source of lighting was still in use in 1945. Mains water was also brought from the city supply at Pinhoe and Lord Poltimore had this extended to the village. The ancient drain for sewage running under the house was replaced by a new external drain, although water continued to run through the original system which eventually found its way into the Clyst river. This

ABOVE

Thistle and ragwort in Poltimore's garden

flow of water was said never to cease even in the driest of summers.

Much of the 1st Baron's renovations were obscured by his son's additions of 1908. The semi-circular portico looking over the park towards the Chinese Garden was removed when the new wing was built, comprising the Green Drawing Room, later the Ballroom, Lord Poltimore's study and a Morning Room, and Lady Poltimore's suite of rooms above. The oak floor of the Ballroom, hung on chains, was reputed to be the best dance floor in Devon and, with its fine white chimneypiece panelled in Sienna marble and lit by the newly installed electric chandeliers, was the scene of many balls and seasonal festivities. This wing of the house suffered huge damage when arsonists tried to destroy the house in 1987. Augustus and Florence did not, however, live to enjoy their new house for long; he died in 1908 and Lady Poltimore the following year.

The grandeur of Edwardian aristocratic life at Poltimore House ended with the outbreak of war in 1914. Men went from the village to fight; twelve lost their lives and are commemorated on a plaque inside the church—amongst them these names well known in Poltimore: Victor Turton (Leicestershire Regiment), Arthur Pugsley (Devons) and Charles, Francis and Frank Westcott, all of the Devon Regiment and who may all have come from the same family. The number of lives lost in the First World War is in stark contrast to the one casualty sustained between 1939 and 1945—Thomas Tozer RAFVR, of Hayes Barton, who was killed in 1942.

Two lucky survivors of the First World War were Robert Stark, captain of the Poltimore Football Team, who had married Hilda Lindsay, daughter of George Lindsay, Lord Poltimore's gamekeeper,

and Samuel Brooks, who worked on the Poltimore estate, rather as a Jack-of-all-trades, helping with the horses and in the saw mills and sometimes taking surplus fruit and vegetables to a market on the outskirts of Exeter. Samuel Brooks also acted as a beater for shooting parties, a coveted job at that time and, according to his daughter Doris May Graham, was required to sleep in the 'big house' when Lord and Lady Poltimore were away, as the staff wouldn't sleep there by themselves. He joined the Coldstream Guards, going off to war when Doris May was a baby. She remembers him returning from France after the Armistice, seeing him walk down the lane in his uniform and wondering at the strange man who was coming into their house! Doris Brooks helped in Poltimore House with odd jobs, not getting paid but being given free teas. She often acted as 'ball boy' at tennis parties at Poltimore and nearby Killerton House and sang in the church choir, the girls in the front row of pews segregated from the boys who sat in the choir stalls. At Christmas everyone went to parties at the House and there were games and dancing and wonderful food. There was, of course, no alcohol. Lord Poltimore was very strict on that subject and had earlier closed down a cider house in the village when he surprised some of his workers 'under the influence'. At Christmas anyone resident in Poltimore village who worked at the House was given a blanket (the Brooks family had four),

ABOVE

The funeral of Lady Poltimore in 1909. The coffin being carried up the lime avenue preceded by Poltimore church choir and followed by family and friends

but there was some bad feeling about this gift in the surrounding villages, because those who worked at the House but lived at, say, Huxham or Broadclyst, did not receive a blanket. However, the estate seems to have had a pension scheme, presumably in operation before 1920, for permanent staff. When Frank Stark, stonemason on the Poltimore estate, died in 1940, the 4th Baron wrote from North Molton sending condolences to the family: 'I remember him well at Poltimore in the old days and I am pleased to know that his pension contributed towards his ease and comfort in his declining years'.

In 1918 the 3rd Baron died; and in 1921 the last event in the history of the Bampfyldes at Poltimore took place when the estate of 1,960 acres was put up for sale. Although the mansion itself and the grounds (although let) remained in the 4th Lord Poltimore's ownership until 1944, the Bampfyldes' long occupation of the 'Pool by the Great House' had come to an end.

BELOW

A Poltimore village wedding group, probably of the Holmes family. Mr Holmes, 4th from left in back row, was wheelwright, smith, cider maker, undertaker and coachbuilder

Here lies the body of William Fodoe, late Coachman to Sir Richard Warwick Bampfylde Bart, in whose service he died October 18th, 1752, aged 42.

Coachman! Yet Foe to Drink, of Heart sincere,
In manners gentle and in Judgement clear;
Safe thro' ye chekerd Track of Life he drove.
And gained ye Treasure of his master's love;
Upright his carriage; moved with wondrous skill;
Nor stopped but when ye Wheels of Life stood still.
Here now he lies, expecting that Reward
The faithfull servant merits from his Lord.'

By direction of The Right Honourable LORD POLTIMORE, D.L. and J.P.

EXETER - DEVON.

Illustrated Particulars, Plan and Conditions of Sale

OF

The Poltimore Park Estate

A Compact and Highly Attractive - -
Residential, Agricultural and Sporting Property

Under five miles from the Important City of Exeter and a little
over two miles from Pinhoe Station on the L. & S.W. Railway
(Main Line), comprising

The Stately Early Georgian Mansion

CONTAINING

SPACIOUS HALL, 7 RECEPTION ROOMS, BILLIARD ROOM,
46 BED ROOMS, 7 BATH ROOMS and DOMESTIC OFFICES.

Standing in the midst of an UNDULATING PARK of 200 ACRES, beautifully Timbered.

Superb Pleasure Grounds and Gardens, Stabling, Garage, Horticultural
and other Buildings

TOGETHER WITH

Five Excellent Farms

SMALL HOLDING, ACCOMMODATION LAND, COTTAGES
and upwards of 265 ACRES of WOODLANDS

Embracing an Area of about

1,960 Acres.

WHICH

Messrs. COLLINS & COLLINS

Will Sell by Auction, in Several Lots,
AT "THE ROUGEMONT HOTEL," EXETER,

On Friday, the 23rd day of September, 1921,

At TWO o'clock precisely (unless previously disposed of by Private Treaty).

Particulars, Plan and Conditions of Sale may be obtained from Messrs. RICCARD & SON,
Solicitors, South Molton, North Devon; or of the Auctioneers,
Messrs. COLLINS & COLLINS,

37, South Audley Street,

Telephone: Gerrard 5960.　　　　　　　　Grosvenor Square, London, W.1.

The Pleasures that go with Learning: 1923–1945

The catalogue of the Poltimore estate sale in 1921 states incorrectly that the house dates back to AD 1298, but also observes, more accurately, that it would serve very well (assuming that it were too big to be taken on again as a 'Family Seat') as a 'Residential Hotel, Club, School, Hydro, Hospital or other Public Institution'. And a school, in one form or another, is what it became for the next twenty years. The five farms, amounting to about 1,500 acres, and a few hundred acres of woodland were sold, mostly to the occupying tenants. The Tavender family, for instance, had come from Farringdon in East Devon as tenants of Lord Poltimore at Lathys Farm in 1914 and they now became owners. Their daughter Phyllis married Tom Besley and in turn the Besleys farmed Lathys until their son-in-law, Michael Gibbins took over, and now his son—four generations of the same family, spanning most of the 20th century. The mansion and park, however, together with the pleasure grounds, gardens, stables and other outbuildings, totalling 250 acres, failed to find a buyer and consequently Lord Poltimore leased the property to a girls' boarding school from Wrantage in Somerset.

According to the North Curry Parish Magazine of September 1923, the departure of Newport School from Wrantage was a cause of regret. The children were taken by charabanc to view their new premises in Devon and treated to a strawberries-and-cream tea on trestle tables set outside the main front of the house. They were delighted. The school changed its name to Poltimore College, and the life of the house took on a completely different aspect. The deer still grazed under the oaks in the park, however, looked after by

BELOW

*Poltimore College and
playing fields showing
the newly built chapel*

George Lindsay, and Albert Thorne, who lived at the Old Lodge and became groom to Miss Celia Wontner, the Principal of the School (always known as The Head). The Head brought with her from Wrantage her general factotum, Harold Lane, who settled at The Kennels after George Lindsay died and eventually farmed part of the estate. Many of the original Poltimore staff stayed on to work for the new management; William Aldridge, for instance, who lived at New Lodge, worked as woodman, gardener and blacksmith. In spite of the fact that he had lost his right arm as a result of a circular-saw accident, with a steel hook strapped on the amputated end he was able to drive a tractor, or the pony cart and, most important of all, he was the one man who could fire the temperamental gas engine for generating electricity. William was one of the large family of Aldridge who had come from Hampshire in the 19th century. His sister Florence was the only one of the family not born in Poltimore; she married John Turton of Poltimore and for many years was sexton of the church. Their descendants still live in Poltimore today.

The grounds and gardens were thus kept up by many of the original Poltimore staff, and in term-time at least the population of the parish

of Poltimore was considerably increased. According to accounts given by former pupils of Poltimore College, the girls were allowed no contact with the village, neither at the shop and post office, presided over by the formidable Miss Florence Grant, whose father James Grant had started the service in 1865, at the church, as the College built a chapel, timber-framed and clad and roofed with asbestos, in a space behind the west wing of the house. In this The Head, who came of the theatrical Wontner family, used to preach dramatic sermons, which were listened to with some reverence. One former pupil testifies to the fact that the building, though plain, has remained in her mind as a very holy place. Another, however, at the age of about nine, so hated her first week at Poltimore, and in particular the school breakfasts of bread and porridge, that she climbed out of a downstairs window one morning and ran across the park to New Lodge, where the Aldridges took charge of her and escorted her back to the school. Fortunately, the cuisine improved and the rest of her four years in the splendid surroundings of the house and park are now recollected in tranquillity.

In fact, many former pupils have said that living in such a beautiful place as Poltimore contributed to their schooldays being happy ones. One who was at the College from 1925 to 1928 remembers the feeling of welcome the house gave, and how she was interested in her reaction to that even at a young age. For another, however, the grand staircase held particular memories, for the Head used to hold court there every morning and all those pupils who had misbehaved were lined up on the left side to be suitably admonished—so this pupil, who was invariably in hot water, spent a lot of her time quaking in her shoes on the stairs! There was a great contrast, though, between being taught in lofty classrooms, studying in the school library, installed in the 18th-century white-and-gold Saloon, and passing up and down the grand staircase

TOP

Interior of the chapel

BOTTOM

The entrance hall at Poltimore College in the 1920s

where some of the Bampfylde portraits still hung, and the spartan nature of the dormitories with orange boxes for lockers and only cold water for washing, which of course had ice on it on winter mornings. The prefects, however, had quite cosy studies up in the attics and the wide path in the central avenue of cedars was termed 'the prefects' walk', from which lesser mortals were excluded. The food was never enough, only one decent meal a day, but a twice-yearly treat was roast venison after the cull of the deer. In the autumn they would hear the stags roaring at night and listen to the clashing of their antlers as they fought each other for mates. In the spring they waited for the fawns to appear and had to take care not to step on them concealed in the long grass. These were certainly pleasures in a world rather cut off from daily events, newspapers at that time being the only means of knowing what was going on outside. One former pupil remembers at the time of the General Strike in 1926, a member of the staff returning from Exeter and walking across the park waving a paper and shouting 'the Strike is over!' In 1928 the girls smoked bits of glass in the fire in the Tudor dining room and watched the eclipse of the sun from the parapet. A few boys were included in the early days of the College, having come from Somerset with the original school. The boys sometimes filched cigarettes from the staff and initiated the more daring girls into illegal smoking behind the trees in the park.

ABOVE LEFT

The school library in the Saloon in the 1920s

ABOVE RIGHT

A prefect's study in the Tudor attics

There were many outdoor activities, keeping hens and golden pheasants in the former aviaries—some of the birds, including two Alexander Cranes, remained from Lord Poltimore's day—and even learning to milk cows in the stable yard, where Harold Lane had a shippon for his Guernsey herd. Jack Finnimore, who had been keeper of the aviary for Lord Poltimore in the 1880s only retired in 1932 and,

like other Poltimore men, George Lindsay, gamekeeper, and James and William Aldridge, remained on the staff when Poltimore College was instituted. The Aldridges looked after the main hockey pitch in front of the house, and this was reckoned to be almost the best in Devon and was often used for County matches. Tennis courts were laid out on the east lawns and a swimming pool dug in the stream by the Chinese Garden. The Head indulged her theatrical talents and the College put on performances of *The Mikado*, Edward German's *Merrie England* and *The Admirable Crichton*. Miss Wontner also at one stage decided she was dying of some illness and had her bed put out on a landing and the whole school had to file past and say their farewells. She recovered, of course, but by 1939 the numbers of pupils had run down, the College was in financial difficulties and could no longer afford to pay the resident domestic staff. One former pupil remembers with sadness watching them leave, walking down the drive carrying their suitcases. Thereafter, the College was divided into groups responsible for cleaning the house every morning before lessons and, so reduced were the circumstances, the girls were sometimes detailed to pick bunches of violets from the walled garden for sale in Exeter Market.

In 1939 the College was disbanded and the girls who were not

of leaving age were transferred to other schools. Dover College in Kent, who had had to leave Dover at the outbreak of war and had been housed briefly at Blundells School at Tiverton, descended on Poltimore in 1940, taking over the lease from Lord Poltimore, and remained for the duration. The wartime archives of Dover College record that the house was in a fairly disorganised and dirty state, needing a great deal of sweeping and cleaning, and distempering of many of the rooms. This work was done by some of the former domestic staff who lived in Poltimore village, the Headmaster's wife and the wives of the masters, while even the boys were commandeered to help. The Headmaster, George Renwick, and his family of four children moved into the former coachman's house in one corner of the stable yard. Harold Lane retained his shippons and continued to farm eighty acres of the land that remained in Lord Poltimore's ownership, and his cattle now grazed the park in place of the deer, which had all been culled at the outbreak of war. The boys also worked in the kitchen gardens growing vegetables, particularly potatoes, under the watchful eye of Bill Aldridge and, unlike the girls, they were encouraged to take part in the life of the village, and in the war effort. There was the Home Guard for those over seventeen (one of the Headmaster's cars, he was an avid car collector, with all the doors removed was the squadron vehicle); there was Scouts, apple picking and the OTC with its headquarters and parade ground in the stable yard where the corps of drums and bugles practised hard. In the summer holidays they would go to harvest camps at Braunton in North Devon. At Poltimore the boys had a fair amount of freedom and would bicycle long distances in search of birds' eggs and to fish for trout and grayling in the Exe at Up Exe, once being chased by a keeper for poaching, and pike in the Exeter Canal. Two of the boys reared owls (stealing the eggs from the barns of Lathys Farm) and buzzards—these birds of prey still swoop over the park today.

ABOVE

The Saloon as sixth-form Common Room in the 1940s. Photograph Dover College archives

They kept the chicks in the aviaries behind the house, where Lord Poltimore had displayed his white peacocks and pheasants, and set mousetraps throughout the house to feed them. A tawny owl became tame enough to sit on the handlebars of a bicycle and attend cricket matches and get taken to the summer camps. In winter some of the boys went wildfowling for duck, geese or waders, their guns disguised in hessian wrapping along the cross bars of their bicycles. The results of these forays were subsequently eaten privately or stuffed as specimens, all against school rules. The wartime meat ration being rather small, the boys were always on the lookout for anything edible, and Bill Aldridge taught them to skin rabbits, which they cooked in ovens made from old biscuit tins. Once one of the Headmaster's chickens was caught, cooked in this way and eaten, without anyone in authority finding out. Bill also taught them to catch and skin moles—though what they did with the mole pelts is not reported! Inside the house the main rooms were turned into classrooms, much as they had been during the time of Poltimore College. The Saloon was again used as a library and a common room for the Sixth Form, the Red Drawing Room a classroom and the Ballroom was used for assembly. A series of small rooms off the long passage to the kitchens, (demolished in 2004) and once used as piano-practice rooms by the girls, became sixth-form studies for the boys. The old Laundry in the house was converted to a chemistry laboratory—and turned back into a laundry when Poltimore subsequently became a hospital. The coachhouses in the stable block still housed the generating plant and other bits and pieces of machinery and provided a draw for enthusiastic Dover schoolboys who waited to watch Bill Aldridge start up the engines, using the hook on his arm with great dexterity.

Although the house escaped with no more than a few broken windows when a landmine was dropped just outside the grounds, Poltimore was not untouched by the war. In 1940, soon after RAF Exeter (now Exeter Airport) was opened, a Sector Control Room was established in a concrete blockhouse on the edge of the park alongside the road from Broadclyst. RAF Exeter and its substations in other parts of Devon and Somerset played an active part in the Battle of Britain, the Blitz and the D-Day campaign as well as providing convoy escorts through the Western Approaches and day- and night-fighter cover for

BELOW

The Engine Room in the Stable Block

the towns of the South West, and cities such as Exeter and Plymouth, throughout the war years. The 'ops room' at the Poltimore Park site was key to the collection of information from the Royal Observer Corps and radar stations and airfields, coordinating the response of Exeter's fighter squadrons, AA batteries and searchlight stations and reporting back to Fighter Command group HQ—a vital element in the matter of defence in the early years of the conflict and equally in the successful prosecution of the war after 1944. After 1945, when RAF Exeter was disbanded, the Poltimore site became redundant but was eventually reoccupied by the ROC and remained in use until the 1990s and the ending of the Cold War period. Even after 1945 there were few signs on the surface of the blockhouses being used, one reason being that most of the accommodation was quite deep underground.

None of this would have been known to the boys of Dover College during their wartime sojourn at the House, although they probably knew of the American army unit that, like Cromwell's troops, was briefly camped in the park. But there were other incidents—in 1941 a Wellington bomber crashed in the woods near Pinhoe and the Dover College Fire Brigade went out to help in the rescue. This turned out to be a harrowing experience for the schoolboys, for they found the crew all dead. An Old Dovorian commanded a Polish Spitfire Squadron (317) based at RAF Exeter. He gave his pilots an order that whenever they shot down an enemy aircraft they were to do a 'Victory Roll' over Poltimore House before landing—and this happened many times. In 1942 during the so-called Baedeker raids on Exeter the cellars were used as an air raid shelter, and the boys were taught to practise sliding down ropes slung from the parapet in the event of incendiary bombs landing on the roof while they were asleep in the attic rooms. Another grim reminder of the war came when the whole College was assembled in the chapel to hear George Renwick read out the names of former

ABOVE
Boys doing PE

pupils, some only recently left, who had lost their lives on active service.

The boys went back to Dover at the end of the summer term of 1945—but not before they had played high jinks with the cannon balls, said to date from the Crimean War, which decorated the drive near the main porch. Some of these were dragged up to the attics and flung from the parapet (without doing any damage to life or limb) and one ended up in someone's bed. For most of the boys it had been a good time to look back on in later years; for many of them Poltimore was the only school environment they had known, and at least one has confessed that the return to Dover was a bit of a culture shock! Considering the hard use which the house must have endured during Dover College's tenancy, really very little damage was done—one or two of the marble chimneypieces had got kicked and chipped, and a few fittings and a written history of the house mysteriously disappeared, but on the whole the wear and tear was no more than would have been expected.

By the time the war ended Lord Poltimore had sold the mansion, with 112 acres, to an Exeter timber merchant, and it was then that the park and some of the woodlands were thinned of the best timber. This period of ownership lasted only a short time and was followed by an abortive attempt to turn the house into an hotel. Finally, in October 1945 it was acquired by an Exeter doctor and his doctor wife, who had already foreseen the post-war need for a new hospital in the area and found in Poltimore House the ideal building and surroundings for this purpose.

The Poltimore Hospitals: 1945–1975

The setting-up of a hospital at Poltimore House was not undertaken without consultation with the medical fraternity of Exeter, and there were some who thought the project too ambitious to succeed. However, the need for an extension of the hospital facilities in the city and county immediately after the war was acute and by October 1945 the purchase was completed and work began to prepare for the first patients. The new owner, Dr Richard Fortescue-Foulkes, had practised in Exeter since 1921 and was also anaesthetist at the Royal Devon & Exeter Hospital, the West of England Eye Infirmary and the Princess Elizabeth Orthopaedic Hospital. He leased the house to a private company, Poltimore House Ltd, of which he became Managing Director and Secretary, and a senior Exeter ophthalmic surgeon, Mr Michael Dykes Bower, was appointed Chairman. The proprietor's wife, Dr Mary Fortescue-Foulkes, had also practised in Exeter from 1921 to 1940 and was medical officer in the Casualty Department of the Royal Devon & Exeter Hospital during the war. She became Housekeeper at Poltimore and later Resident Medical Officer. Richard and Mary Foulkes retained the former Red Drawing Room looking out on to the park for their private use, together with the adjoining Saloon on the east front, which was occasionally used for receiving the relatives of patients; an office for administrative purposes at the foot of the 17th-century staircase and two upper rooms and bathroom—the former Parlour Chamber and Hall Chamber of the Tudor wing. Like many occupants of Poltimore House before and since, the attraction of the place soon took a hold

OPPOSITE
Poltimore House in the 1970s with chimneys shortened

62

on the new owners, and there was a positive attempt to make the house feel, on entering it, more like a family home than an institution.

A feature of the estate was the small octagonal building of 1831, Old Lodge, at the north-east entrance, known after the introduction of the multi-sided coin in 1936 as the Threepenny Lodge. The lodge was offered as rent-free accommodation for the hospital cook and her daughter and together with all other buildings connected with the property was included in the Company's twenty-one year lease. The only exclusion was part of the stable block, which was still let to Harold Lane who continued to farm eighty acres of the land. Polly, the bay mare inherited with the property, was also stabled there and looked after by Bill Aldridge, and a pony trap acquired. For a year or two, while petrol rationing was still in force, this conveyance was used by members of the family or staff to fetch supplies for the hospital from Martin Gibbins, the family butcher in Broadclyst. Before

ABOVE
Old Lodge in 1958

the motorway was built it was a pleasant ride through the lanes to Broadclyst and back with rounds of beef, legs of lamb and sides of pork. Bill and his father, James Aldridge, also maintained the lawns on the east side of the house, with the help of Polly who drew the mowing and raking machines, and a tennis court and croquet lawn were kept mown for the use of the nursing staff. Horse power was also used in the woodlands to clear the ground of laurel scrub, the timber dragged out of the undergrowth by chains, with 'whippers' to protect the horse's hind legs, and loaded onto a butt cart to be cut up for logs for the many fires kept going in the house. The circular-saw bench in the stable yard was still powered by one of the gas engines even after mains electricity arrived in the late 1940s, but the logs were cut by hand. Mowing between the trees in the woodland was carried out in dry weather, Polly harnessed to an old style reaper with one heavy drive wheel, with a seat over for the operator. This was hard work for a fifteen-hand horse, and a Fordson tractor was later acquired but not much used as it was difficult to start, and in the end Polly proved the better bet. Apart from her other qualities, this

BELOW

Raking the paths with Polly in the 1950s

amiable animal was a useful saddle horse. Although the lawns and woodlands were generally maintained and rose beds created on the north side of the house, there was no attempt to return to the formal gardening plan of the early 20th century with its long herbaceous beds in the central walk. All this would have required enormous upkeep, and the key outdoor staff were fully employed elsewhere in the grounds. Many bulbs were planted, however, and these, mostly daffodils, have now spread throughout the woodlands. Primroses and violets abound in spring and, in some years, bluebells. In about 1950 four saplings were planted round the perimeter of the east lawn, all interesting specimens chosen to enhance the immediate environment of the house. The first was *Amelanchier laevis*, noted for its white flowers which are followed by red berries and then brilliant coloured foliage in autumn; the second a Japanese Paper Bark Maple *Acer griseum*, with distinctive, cinnamon-coloured bark; and the third the spectacular *Davidia involucrata*, commonly known as the Handkerchief Tree, the first seeds of which were brought back from China by Ernest Wilson for the Veitch nurseries in 1902. The fourth sapling was a deciduous conifer, *Metasequoia glyptostroboides* or Dawn Redwood, a

magnificent tree that, after the sale of Poltimore House to the Regional Hospital Board, was dug up and replanted in North Devon. All these specimens came from the Veitch Nursery, which was then still in operation in Exeter.

At the stables, the coachman's house where the Headmaster of Dover College had lived during the war, was let to Edward Franklin, elder son of Herbert Franklin who had started his working life as a stable boy at Poltimore House in the time of the 2nd Baron. The Franklins set up a vegetable-growing business in the kitchen garden and at the beginning supplied some of the

OPPOSITE
*The Handkerchief Tree (*Davidia involucrata*) in May 2004.*

BELOW
The north front in 2000

needs of the hospital. A young member of the Foulkes family, on demobilisation from the WRNS, kept a small herd of dairy goats in the unused part of the stables and ran a milk round in the Poltimore–Huxham area while milk supplies were still under wartime restrictions.

Inside the house much alteration and reconstruction was necessary. A great deal of the work took up to two years to complete and the members of the various contracting firms became well known to the hospital staff and patients, usually sharing in festivities such as Christmas. There were altogether 75 rooms and the number was now increased to 80 by subdivision. On the ground floor the former Library became a surgical ward known as Bampfylde Ward, and the connecting Ballroom gave accommodation for ten medical cases. Named Harvey Ward after William Harvey, the 17th-century physician who first correctly described the mechanism of the heart and the circulation of the blood, this room's space, light and quiet surroundings made it an ideal hospital ward. The two large rooms joining the ballroom were used as a room for the Matron and a sitting

ABOVE

Poltimore as a hostpital in the 1950s

room for the nursing staff. On the north-east side the Billiard Room, in Tudor times the kitchen of the house, was converted to an up-to-date operating theatre unit—a task that presented many problems. The walls had to be stripped of all the old plaster and the whole room, as also the rooms to be used for anaesthetics and sterilising, lined with terrazzo. This highly skilled work was carried out by a family of Italian craftsmen from South Devon, whose methods of laying this type of pavement were closely guarded secrets. During the process of conversion of this room a massive fireplace and stone lintel were uncovered, with traces of five succeeding fireplaces, each smaller than the preceding one, as well as the outline of an archway—possibly the entrance to Richard Bampfylde's original 16th-century building. The illuminated screen for viewing X-rays during operations was sited over the centre of this fireplace, the ventilation of the chimney being used to keep the screen cool. There are probably not many instances of a Tudor chimney being put to this use! The surgical unit was officially opened on 8th January 1948 and the first operation performed was, appropriately, an emergency Caesarean delivery. The theatre, anaesthetic room and sterilising unit were latterly under the

BELOW

The former Ballroom as Harvey Ward in the 1950s

supervision of Fred Wollacott who had started work at Poltimore in the first days of the hospital with the job of porter and general factotum.

In spite of the upheaval of conversion and renovation it was possible to admit a small number of patients as early as 8th November 1945. The first baby was born in the maternity unit on the first floor on 7th January 1946, and this set the pattern for several years. Upstairs there were seven private rooms for maternity cases and ten beds in two wards kept under contract to Devon County Council, a very valuable arrangement after the war when the birth rate rose rapidly. Up to 1960, when the maternity department was closed, 1,401 babies were born at Poltimore, a greater number than the total in the parish of Poltimore for the preceding 300 years. Altogether 10,013 patients were admitted during the years 1945 to 1963, of which 4,674 were National Health Service patients. In its first fifteen years as a medical institution Poltimore certainly helped towards the reduction of the hospital waiting list. Hip replacement using a silver ball was an operation which was pioneered by Norman Capener, a senior Exeter orthopaedic surgeon, at Poltimore in the 1950s.

The atmosphere of the house, remembered by many of the girls and boys who had spent their schooldays at Poltimore, seems to have been equally recalled by the next occupants—the patients and staff of the hospitals. The hall, in spite of a receptionist's desk and small telephone exchange in one corner, where Phyllis Barnard ('Physs' as she was known to everybody) reigned supreme for many years, still looked more like the entrance to a country house than a hospital. At Christmas the centre of the hall was taken up by a huge, decorated fir tree. The big iron stove was kept burning in the winter and staff and patients often sat round it, while the imperial staircase so impressed one visiting grandmother that she insisted on carrying her newborn grandchild down it, much to the chagrin of Matron whose prerogative it was to take the babies going home to the front door. Occasionally things went wrong; two cousins with the same surname had their babies at the same time and nearly got mixed up, only a distinguishing birthmark on one baby preventing a case of mistaken identity. But then, this was a case of history repeating itself, for was not the 16th-century builder of Poltimore House, Richard Bampfylde, himself a twin, only rescued from an untimely fate by his distinguishing birthmark? Unbelievably, smoking was allowed in the rooms and wards during the day, each bed having an ashtray on the locker! The view from the windows overlooking the park was often remarked on by patients, who

could in the early days watch cricket matches on the grass fronting the house and, until about 1953, red squirrels running through the trees.

In 1946 one of the directors of the hospital board who had been a TB sufferer early in her medical career, offered to manage a Thoracic Unit by converting the former chapel wing into a ward for twelve thoracic patients. Architects' draft plans were drawn up and a great deal of discussion with senior consultants in Exeter took place as to the viability of this proposal. One opinion held that if accommodation for twenty cases could be provided, the siting of a new unit for treating diseases of the chest proposed for the Devon and Cornwall subregion of the South West Regional Hospital Board would most likely be made at Poltimore House. In the end nothing came of this scheme, mainly because the original proposer declared herself unable to recruit and hold together the specialist staff of nurses that would be required. The final decision not to go ahead with this sort of mini-sanatorium at Poltimore was made towards the end of 1947—just before the National Health Service came into being. The Ministry of Health had also stated that all licences for work on medical institutions were to be stopped—and this finally put paid to any alterations to the chapel at Poltimore.

The daily running of Poltimore House Ltd was not without problems. There were major headaches on the financial side of things, which improved after 1950, but minor problems, in the early days were often surmounted by a mixture of ad hoc methods and a certain amount of goodwill; for instance, some of the night nursing staff were not resident, but came out nightly from Exeter on the bus which dropped them at 9 pm at The Bowls, on the main Pinhoe to Broadclyst road.

ABOVE LEFT

Fred Wollacott (theatre attendant) and Phyllis Barnard (receptionist) in the 1950s

ABOVE RIGHT

Sister Page, photograph of c. 1954

It was a long walk in the dark or in bad weather even by the short cut across the park to the house, so an informal car service had to be operated, either by the proprietors themselves or any member of their family or friends staying who would drive, and 'fetching the nurses' became a routine interruption in the course of the evening.

The resident nurses slept up in the attics over the west wing, reached by a small staircase, a part of the house not connected with the Tudor attics. A junior nurse who looked after the babies who were left for adoption or fostering, was paid 7/6d (37 ½p) a week, all found, with 2/6d (12 ½p) towards her bus fare home to North Devon at weekends—not a fortune, and the work had its sad moments, as there was little provision for unmarried mothers fifty years ago.

The hospital cats earned their living and became well known to all the staff and visiting doctors as well as many of the patients. Rainbow, a tortoiseshell female, and one of her black kittens, called Sugar Ray Robinson after the American champion boxer of the 1950s, kept mainly to the kitchen area of the house and were useful mousers. The last incumbent was the inscrutable George, a black and white cat which treated the whole of the ground floor of the house as his personal domain and spent every evening in the Red Drawing Room. On being let out at night by the main front door, he regularly spat at the base of one of the pillars in the hall. When the floor-boards above this pillar had to be taken up for some electrical repairs the skeleton of a cat was found, presumably the object of George's distaste!

By 1958 Richard and Mary Foulkes were beginning to think of retirement, and although the property did not pass out of their hands until 1963, they moved to North Devon from where they commuted to Poltimore several times a week. A new resident medical officer (Dr E Squires) was appointed, and for some years he and his family enjoyed the splendid surroundings of the house as others had done before them. BUPA had already made overtures about taking over Poltimore either on a lease

BELOW

The west wing of Poltimore House in the 1970s under the ownership of the Regional Hospital Board. Note removal of parapet and chimney stacks. Photograph Arthur Luxton

or as new owners. Nothing came of this idea, but in the summer of 1962 the sale of the property was agreed to the South West Regional Hospital Board, who had been involved in the leasing of beds from the Company more or less from the outset. Poltimore House Ltd was voluntarily wound up and in 1963 the premises became part of the Exeter Hospitals Group. Poltimore House Ltd had been a rewarding enterprise, though not necessarily in a financial sense, but the gloomy forebodings expressed by some had not materialised and Poltimore remained a medical establishment under the NHS until the new Royal Devon and Exeter Hospital was built at Wonford.

During the Regional Hospital Board's time at Poltimore several alterations were made to both the exterior and interior of the house. The balustraded parapet running round the entire building except for

the northeast and northwest gabled façades was removed, together
with most of the chimneys, and the attic windows once more exposed
on the south and east fronts. This returned the house to the way it had
looked in the 1820s and was perhaps an improvement; the iron gates
of the porch were also removed and the porch glazed; this was a less
sympathetic alteration, although no doubt done for practical reasons.
A passenger lift was installed at one side of the main staircase—again
a necessary, but hardly an aesthetic, addition to the grand proportions
of the staircase. The 17th-century oak staircase
leading to the tower was unfortunately painted, while
a great loss during this period of ownership was
some of the fine plaster ceilings already described.
The Hospital Board sold the property in 1975.

Two Decades of Disaster: 1976–1997

The potential of a building on the scale of Poltimore House, set in parkland and easily accessible from the city of Exeter, was realized almost as soon as it passed out of the hands of the Bampfyldes. We have seen how it adapted to housing two schools and two medical institutions in succession, and by the mid1970s, when it again became vacant, there should have been grounds for hoping this kind of use would be continued. Events, however, turned out to be quite different and the following twenty years brought one disaster after another.

The Health Authority put the property on the market in 1975. From an historical standpoint their decision to sell it in different lots was unfortunate, and resulted in the house being separated from its wider parkland. Only thirteen acres remained with the mansion, which was soon bought by a local entrepreneur who lived for a short period in the north wing. It then passed into the ownership of Hans Jurgen Abel who ran it as a convalescent home. The regulating authority, Devon County Council, would only permit twenty-four residents and this made the business impossible to sustain, given the size of the house and the funds needed for its upkeep. In 1986 the house was repossessed by the Portsmouth Building Society.

The act of repossession triggered off a bizarre episode in the history of Poltimore House that deeply shocked not only the residents of Poltimore village, but anyone who had past connections with the house and estate. In the summer of 1987, during the small hours of the morning, a local farmer saw flames coming from the direction of the house. The property had been empty since the repossession, with

BELOW

*The southwest aspect
of Poltimore showing
the extent of the damage
sustained by fire in the
1908 wing of the house
in 1987*

only a caretaker living in part of the ground floor. He fortunately escaped injury in the fire, which started in the ground floor of the west wing and spread to the whole of that side of the house. The damage was enormous and estimated to be about £300,000. It was the beginning of a most unhappy chapter in the history of the house.

The fire, as it turned out, had been started deliberately. In September 1987 at Wonford Magistrates Court the previous owner was charged, together with an Exeter man, with conspiring to cause a fire without lawful excuse. Another man was also charged with the latter, with conspiracy to cause a fire. At their trial at Exeter Crown Court the owner of the house was acquitted of the charge, while one of the other men turned Queen's Evidence and received a suspended sentence; the third was jailed for two-and-a-half years. The result of this arson was that the house became immediately vulnerable to theft and vandalism. Notwithstanding, in 1988 a London-based development company took out a mortgage of £500,000 with Skipton

Building Society, a mortgage personally guaranteed by the company's managing director. The company's proposal was to add a vast extension to the house and a complex of apartments, and it produced architects' plans. English Heritage, however, who were involved because of the building's Grade 2 status, rejected the scheme. The meeting with English Heritage and East Devon District Council to discuss these proposals took place in 1988.

By the following year East Devon District Council were becoming increasingly concerned about the deteriorating condition of the property. The Council served an Urgent Works Notice on the company, which required the owner to carry out works to secure the building. No response to this requirement was received and East Devon District Council therefore completed the essential repairs and billed the development company for £25,000.

In 1989/90 the developer produced a new set of architects' plans to convert the house into a £6 million hotel and conference centre. Full planning permission and listed building consent was granted in 1991 for the project. There was, however, a legal agreement attached to the grant of the permission that required the main house to be restored before the development took place. The agreement also required the owner to effect immediate emergency repairs. As we have seen, the building was becoming increasingly vulnerable to weather, theft and vandalism. The developer did in fact instruct a local building firm to felt and batten the roof, but the work was not completed owing to non-payment of bills; as it turned out, what was done did more harm than good. It was the first and last work carried out by the supposed owner.

Had Poltimore House been sited in a remote part of the country, away from public view or any large centre of population, it would not have survived the years of neglect that followed; thieves, and the elements, would have reduced its value and its desirability as an object for renovation and restoration until all that remained would

ABOVE

Damaged staircase after the fire in 1987

have been a heap of stone in a wilderness of weeds. Indeed by 1992 the building had deteriorated further and, failing a purchaser with money and vision, descent into ruin and eventual demolition could easily have been its fate. Even its prime location and historic connections with Devon and the city of Exeter might not have saved it had not East Devon District Council assumed responsibility for emergency repair measures on the small budget that was available. From the beginning of their involvement with Poltimore House the District Council's intention was that the building be restored to some beneficial use without losing its special architectural and historic interest. The burden fell on the Council's Principal Planning Officer, Alan Payne, who was to become all too familiar with the problems that surrounded the property for the next seven years. He was supported in this somewhat lonely task by John Vallender, Chief Executive, David Gibbons, Chairman of the Environment and Planning Committee and by Derek Button, a local Councillor, who later became Chairman of Poltimore House Trust. The Council was greatly encouraged and helped by Angela Browning, MP for Tiverton, the constituency in which Poltimore then fell, and then there was the genuine desire of the residents of Poltimore village to see a future for the derelict house—a phoenix rising from the ashes.

As the District Council had been backed by Devon County Council and English Heritage in the initial stages of making the building secure, recompense was now demanded from the company, but the full amount was never received and at the end of the year East Devon District Council took out a County Court action against the company in Westminster County Court. The company was not represented in court and in fact by June 1992 had been struck off the Register of Companies.

On the dissolution of the company, the title of Poltimore House became 'escheated', or handed over to the Crown, and became part of the Crown Estate. This act in the case of Poltimore House was a rare example of the use of the doctrine of the Sovereign being paramount landlord—a feudal law belonging to the 14th rather than the 20th century. In view of the liabilities attached to the building, the Crown disclaimed all rights of ownership or possession under the provisions of the Crown Proceedings Act 1947. The Skipton Building Society was not prepared to release the charge on the building, which by now was nearing the £1 million mark, and

to cooperate in the sale of an unencumbered freehold. This put
Poltimore House in a state of limbo where no one could be found
willing to accept responsibility. Compulsory purchase under the
Planning (Listed Buildings and Conservation Areas) Act 1990 was
now not an option open to the Local Authority as Crown property
cannot be so purchased. The process of escheatment also meant
that the Crown could only convey the property to a new purchaser
on payment of the charge, there being no provision in the Act for
taking action against the owner of a charge on an historic building.

Other people had their eyes on Poltimore House however, and
thefts continued; two major break-ins occurred on separate nights
in December 1993 when the floorboards of the Saloon, the Red
Drawing Room and the bedroom above it were removed. The 1st
Baron Poltimore's grand staircase had already been stolen in a daring
raid and at various times the mahogany doors of the Saloon and
chimneypieces from other ground floor rooms had disappeared,
as had most of the fireplaces from both upstairs and downstairs.
(Subsequently some of the artefacts were retrieved and are in safe
keeping today.) The security system that the District Council had
installed earlier (funded by English Heritage) was by this time proving
too expensive to maintain and was removed and taken to Haldon

Belvedere, another important Devon landmark which has now been
fully restored, but which was then in a similar precarious position to
Poltimore House. At one stage in this period 'New Age' travellers
moved into the park and installed two caravans at the back of the
house, away from public view. At first they were allowed to stay as it was
thought that they might act as watchdogs, and they did not seem to be
doing anything more unlawful than walking off with a few brace of
pheasants which they openly hung on their vehicles. This small group
of travellers carried out some minor works to the building in return
for being allowed to stay, while their presence acted as a deterrent to
further intruders. They were, however, overwhelmed one day by a
larger and most unruly group of travellers. Fights broke out, and the
Police were persuaded to use the Public Order Act to evict both groups.

Throughout 1994 continued efforts were made by East Devon
District Council, and in particular by Alan Payne, to keep the fabric
of Poltimore House from damage as far as it was possible with a
small budget; for instance, he had a fund for the purchase of plastic
buckets which were placed strategically all over the interior of the
house and which had to be emptied fairly frequently. Dry rot made its
appearance at the foot of the Tudor staircase, but the fact that there
was so much air circulating through this huge building, although it

ABOVE

*Gabled 16th century
north front in 2003.
Photograph Rikky
Apps*

82

was boarded up, helped to keep some of the infestations at bay—for the present at least. Meanwhile, early in the year Crispin Manners had bought the former stables, the residence now known as *Poltimore Gardens* and new, locked gates at the entrance to the drive were installed. The mere presence of a family, constantly using the drive and passing in front of the derelict mansion, and who were the only other key-holders of the gates apart from Alan Payne, provided much needed extra security.

Outside parties had been exerting pressure on Government and other bodies for some time in the case of Poltimore House. Here Angela Browning MP played a very helpful role; such was the local interest in Poltimore House that she once complained she could not go shopping on a Saturday morning without her constituents rushing up to ask her about the property! Thanks to her influence, in September 1994 a meeting was held at the Department of National Heritage, attended by representatives of that department, the Crown Estate Commission, the Treasury Solicitor's Department, English Heritage, the Architectural Heritage Fund, Devon County Council and East Devon District Council. After the meeting had been told that Skipton Building Society appeared to be about to make a deal with the owner of the original development company, the discussion turned mainly on the problems associated with property escheated to the Crown; and little was resolved by the end of this short meeting—all of which was a great disappointment to the Local Authority officers who had made a 300-mile round journey in order to take part. The one positive result was that English Heritage were optimistic about helping the District Council with further emergency repairs to the fabric—which was timely, as burglaries had

ABOVE

The 17th-century staircase vandalised in 2004

started again and further items had been taken from the property.

It was with this continuing threat from the successor of the previous failed development company that English Heritage asked the Derbyshire-based Buildings At Risk Trust to intervene. This trust had the reputation of solving the most intractable problems associated with historic buildings. Alan Bemrose, the Secretary of Buildings At Risk Trust (known as BART) managed to persuade the Skipton Building Society to release the charge on Poltimore House for a payment of £60,000. The Crown Estate were only too happy to pass an unencumbered freehold title to BART and, with this accomplished, by Christmas 1996 the problems associated with negligent ownership seemed to be over.

An arrangement was made whereby Alan Payne relinquished his official responsibilities as an officer of the council and became the local representative of BART—but with the use of the facilities of East Devon District Council. With funding from English Heritage, extensive patching was carried out on the main roof of the house, and the 19th-century single-storey buildings in the central courtyard were demolished. This allowed the fabric to 'breathe', and for the first time for many years it afforded a view of the Tudor stairwell. With further funding from the Architectural Heritage Fund BART commissioned a Bristol architect, Niall Philips, to carry out an extensive feasibility study for any future use of the building—which in 1997 by good fortune appeared at last to be on the horizon.

The Millennium and Beyond

In 1997 an arts-based project, The Centre for Contemporary Art and the Natural World (known as CCANW) under the direction of Clive and Jill Adams, had just withdrawn from negotiating a site for their headquarters in North Devon and were looking for a new location. Their vision was to create a centre to explore society's changing relationship to nature through the arts. The Arts Council Lottery Fund (ACE) had awarded Torridge District Council £75,000 for a feasibility study for the plan, and when this site fell through, it was agreed that £20,000 of that grant could be used for an 'options appraisal' study examining other suitable sites. Poltimore House was suggested by the National Trust, owners of the North Devon land and, after considering thirteen other areas in Devon, it was decided to proceed with Poltimore House. Following this, the ACE agreed that East Devon District Council would coordinate a development study, and as a result of an architectural competition, two leading Edinburgh firms, Richard Murphy Architects and Simpson & Brown Architects, were selected to prepare an integrated approach which would conserve the historic building and move it into the 21st century. The new element would be as distinct from Poltimore's 18th-century rebuilding as the 18th-century additions were from Richard Bampfylde's Tudor house. These plans were enthusiastically supported by English Heritage.

In 1998 Buildings At Risk Trust applied to English Heritage for a repair grant of £480,000 for Poltimore House; this was rejected because of uncertainties relating to the end user, and by 1999 BART had become increasingly concerned about the lack of a solution

OPPOSITE
The derelict south front in spring 2004

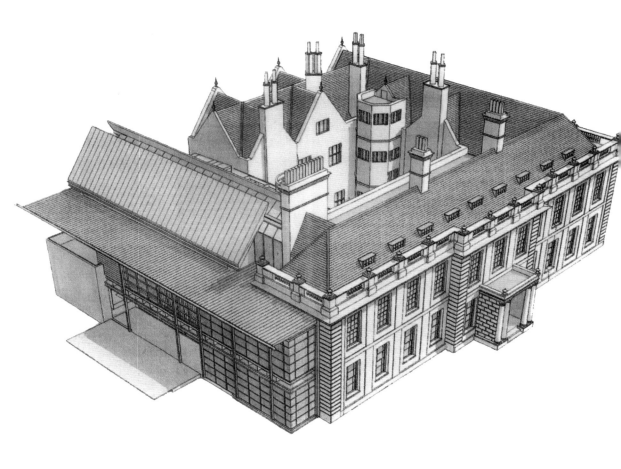

to the use of the house. Their proposal was to put it on the open market, but English Heritage and all those concerned were convinced that the property could not withstand another cycle of commercial speculation and instead suggested the setting up of a wholly independent Poltimore House Trust. The Trust was established early the following year with Alan Payne as Secretary. His first job was to recruit a cross-section of people suitably qualified—and enthusiastic—to act as Trustees. Nine were initially appointed, Derek Button became the first Chairman and monthly meetings began in Exeter in the spring of 2000. The Trust acquired the freehold of the property, received charitable status, and declared its main aim to be the restoration and re-use of Poltimore House with public access to the historic parts and grounds a major consideration. A quarterly newsletter was instituted, the mailing list growing from an initial 50 in 2000 to nearly 900 by 2004. With the publicity that these activities generated, enquiries and donations began to arrive from various parts of the country, and indeed from across the world—notably from former pupils of Poltimore College (1923–1939) and Dover College (1940–1945) and from members of the nursing staff, as well as from patients and their relatives, dating from the hospital era (1945–1975). Two restricted funds were set up at the instigation of former members of the schools, one by Poltimore College to help restore the 17th-century staircase and one by the Old Dovorian Association to reinstate the chimneypiece in the 18th-century Saloon.

Whatever grants or loans might be got in the future by an end-user, it became obvious that even small-scale fundraising was going to be essential to keep the regeneration of Poltimore House in the public eye. In April 2000, as part of a Poltimore village millennium celebration, the Wardour Garrison, a Living History group, was invited to set up their camp in the grounds of the house for three nights and re-enact

BELOW

A group of Old Poltimore College and Dover College pupils and former Poltimore Hospital staff and patients outside the main door in 2002 following the BBC Restoration filming

the negotiation and signing of the Treaty of Exeter which had taken place at Poltimore on 9th April, 1646. This was a joint venture by Poltimore Parish Council, CCANW and Poltimore House Trust, and proved to be a highly successful event enjoyed by over 700 visitors. A photographic exhibition was held in Poltimore Community Hall the same afternoon, covering the history of the House in pictures, also displaying the new architects' plans for the development of the house by Richard Murphy and Simpson & Brown for CCANW. The owner of the woodlands adjoining the Poltimore arboretum opened up the path from the House to Poltimore Church, which was also open to the public all day. This 'open day' was a pointer to what could be achieved for future public access to the house and grounds.

In January 2001 CCANW submitted an application to the Arts Council for £2,500,000 from a total capital scheme of £11,170,000. In the event of this application being successful, East Devon District Council Lottery Funding Working Party recommended a grant of £461,000 as partnership funding to CCANW. A separate application by CCANW (inter-dependent with the Arts Council application) to the Heritage Lottery Fund for £4,872,720 to be used for the historic building out of the total capital scheme of £11,170,000 was made in April 2001.

In June 2001 the Arts Council announced that 60 capital projects worth £90 million had been admitted to their programme, but the South West was amongst the three lowest regions in England to benefit, and only two capital projects in Devon, Somerset and Cornwall were to be supported—and Poltimore House was not one of them. As a result, CCANW had to withdraw its inter-dependent application to

ABOVE
Scenes from the Wardour Garrison's enactment of 1646, April 2000

89

the Heritage Lottery Fund and in December submitted a new one for £6,800,000 towards restoring the historic parts of the house and the new build part of the regeneration plan. For various reasons, mainly financial ones, this application was turned down by the HLF in July 2002.

The problems faced by CCANW in obtaining funds from the Arts Council and Heritage Lottery Fund were not helped by the long delays between consultations. The strategy of the Arts Lottery in particular changed from support for something as bold and imaginative as CCANW's plans for Poltimore to avoiding anything where there was a risk, especially concerning financial viability. Poltimore House Trust meanwhile continued to regard CCANW as the only visible end-user for the house, although the Trust was powerless to influence the outcome as far as the Lottery bodies were concerned.

The end of 2002, however, brought a ray of hope for Poltimore. BBC2 commissioned Endemol, a well-known production company, to produce a new BBC2 series entitled *Restoration*, highlighting the plight of thirty historic buildings 'at risk' in the UK. For the series, which was to be shown in the summer of 2003, the country was divided into ten regions with three buildings in each region, the

programme being in the form of a competition to be decided by public vote at the end of the series with a money prize dependent on the number of votes cast. On the advice of English Heritage, Poltimore House was chosen to be one of the three contestants in the South West, along with Arnos Vale Cemetery in Bristol and Whitfield Tabernacle in Somerset. Griff Rhys Jones was the overall presenter, and he spent a day at Poltimore with a group comprising representatives of both schools and both hospitals together with members of Poltimore House Trust and Simpson & Brown, the conservation architects. Each building also had its own 'champion' and Joan Bakewell CBE was chosen to fly the flag for Poltimore House. She subsequently became Patron of the Friends of Poltimore House.

Although Poltimore received enough votes (69,000) in the first round of voting to get a place in the final, the triumph of the Victoria Baths in Manchester over all other contestants was probably a foregone conclusion. The final took place at the Tower of London in mid-September and was attended by enthusiasts for the cause from Devon, together with Derek Button and Alan Payne, Chairman and Secretary of Poltimore House Trust and supporters from London and Edinburgh. Nevertheless, in spite of missing a financial reward, the programme put Poltimore House in the spotlight in no small way. Added to this, the Trustees had already decided to open as much of the house to the public as was deemed safe, and for eight Sunday afternoons up to the last day of voting, hundreds of visitors queued in brilliant sunshine (or, on one occasion in pouring rain) for a chance to view the interior of a house that for the last twenty years had been locked, shuttered and hidden from public view. Over 2000 names were recorded in the Visitors Book during this period.

During 2003 it became gradually clear that, saving a miracle, the strategy of inter-dependent Lottery bids applied for by CCANW was not achieving its goal. The amounts of money available were becoming less and the policy of the Arts Council had not favoured innovative, but undoubtedly costly, projects such as CCANW at Poltimore House. Had Poltimore House been a winner in the Restoration programme, there could have been a different result, and it was by reason of the timing of the BBC programme that the final decision on whether CCANW should withdraw from the project or not was postponed until after the competition ended in September 2003.

The enormous interest generated in Poltimore House in part by the Restoration programme led to the formation of the Friends of Poltimore House in 2004. The core of the Friends has been formed from those already mentioned who had some long standing interest in the House itself, and they have been joined by many Devon and Exeter residents who are specifically interested in the conservation of this historic building and its environment. An informal meeting was held at Broadclyst on February 14 chaired by Councillor Trevor Cope, and on

92

a Saturday morning very soon after this a group of enthusiasts met at Poltimore House for an inaugural working party in the grounds. A committee of Friends was soon formed under the Chairmanship of Keith Weedon, with a Secretary and Treasurer, and much of the work hitherto carried out by the Trust, such as the circulation of the quarterly Newsletter, was taken over by the Friends. This volunteer group has continued to carry out sterling work in the grounds, clearing the tangled areas around the house, pruning and cutting, topping and mowing the grassed areas and making new pathways. Because of continued break-ins it has also been necessary to renew security shuttering and boarding in many parts of the house, and in this work the carpentry skills of a dedicated group of Friends have been invaluable. This was particularly so after a serious bout of vandalism occurred in October 2004. A very comprehensive photographic record of the house since the formation of the Friends has been put together by Rikky Apps, and new ideas for fundraising are constantly being sought.

A great deal of the outdoor work was completed in time for a one day

LEFT
The 17th-century stair tower. Photograph Rikky Apps

Plant Sale held in the grounds in April and which proved an enormous success—for the 20 specialist nurseries from Devon and Cornwall who took part, for the 1500 visitors and for the Trust and Friends of Poltimore House. This event encouraged the Friends to hold Open Days on Sunday afternoons in June, July, August and September. Because of its present derelict state the house could not be open to the public. This was not a deterrent; the arboretum laid out in the 19th century with its now mature, fine trees, its wildlife—the unexpected flash of a jay's wing, or the white rump of a roe deer (for they now live freely in the environs of the house) and its air of general tranquillity, has brought scores of visitors, some for the first time, to the realisation of what lies behind the now ruinous facade of this historic house. Much may be discovered, or re-discovered by future generations. Shadows of the 17th century formal gardens remain under the lawns where games were played in modern times. Influences of the Enlightenment, so telling in the fabric of the mansion house, seem to have faded in the 'outdoors', or are still to be found. The obligatory flower borders of the Victorians, turned over to cabbages in 1940 were later returned to Nature, and since then the gardens have mercifully escaped the tweakings of 20th century horticultural fads and fancies.

There is at present no successor to the CCANW plans which foundered in 2003 and Poltimore House remains a 'building at risk'. For more than two decades the ravages of Man and Nature have been unkind and severe. But the Friends of Poltimore House are now a real, physical presence in both the grounds and the building, and actively engaged in fundraising for major works of preservation shortly to be undertaken. The Trust is firmly committed to the regeneration of the building and the restoration of its historic parts for the public good. The great house of the Bampfyldes which put the little village of Poltimore on the map four hundred years ago has yet to play its ultimate role in the life of Devon and the West Country.

LEFT
Keith Weedon, chairman of the Friends of Poltimore House, with the author, 2004

Sources and Acknowledgements

Written Sources

Anne Acland, *A Devon Family: the story of the Aclands*, London: Phillimore, 1981

Bridget Cherry and Nikolaus Pevsner, *The Buildings of England*, London 1989

Jo Cox and John Thorp, *Keystone Report*, 1999

Andy Davey and Catherine Gregan, *Simpson and Brown Draft Conservation Plan*, 2002

R Fortescue-Foulkes, *From Celtic Settlement to 20th Century Hospital : The Story of Poltimore House*, 1971

W G Hoskins, *Devon*, London, 1954

Alexander Jenkins, *History of Exeter*, Exeter 1806

Simon Jenkins, *England's Thousand Best Houses*, London, 2003

Eleanor Kerr, *Hunting Parson : The Life and Times of the Reverend John Russell*, London 1963

Nikolaus Pevsner, *The Buildings of England*, London, 1952

John Prince, *The Worthies of Devon*, 1701

Sue Shephard, *Seeds of Fortune: A Gardening Dynasty*, London, 2003

Walpole Society, *Memoirs of Thomas Jones*, The Walpole Society Vol. 32 1946-1948

Acknowledgements

Clive Adams of Centre for Contemporary Arts and the Natural World

Andy Davey and Catherine Gregan, Simpson & Brown Architects, Edinburgh

Peter Child, Alan Payne and other colleagues of the Poltimore House Trust

John Thorp and Jo Cox, Keystone Historic Building Consultants

The Poltimore House Trust

Contact Poltimore House Trust at:
Poltimore House Trust PO Box 409, Exeter EX4 5WZ.

NEXT PAGE
Partial view of the Rococo Room through mirror